Bill Oddie's
BIRDS
OF BRITAIN & IRELAND

SECOND EDITION

NEW
HOLLAND

CONTENTS

INTRODUCTION

It is 14 years since I wrote the first edition of this book. During that time a lot in the bird world has changed, happily some – perhaps most – of it for the better. It is worryingly undeniable that some species, such as Bullfinches, Tree Sparrows and in some areas even House Sparrows, remain scarce or have become more threatened, to the extent that seeing them has become a rare experience. However, many other birds have become more numerous and widespread, and several – such as Little Egret, Red Kite, Ring-necked Parakeet and Marsh Harrier – are also conspicuous and easy to identify. In nearly all cases, the increases in numbers are due to the efforts of organizations such as the RSPB, Wildfowl and Wetlands Trust, and local and national Wildlife Trusts. One should also not forget individuals (you) who are making their gardens more bird friendly by putting out food and planting 'for wildlife'.

The biggest change of all, though, is that birds have become more easy to identify. This is not because they have simplified their plumage, or drawn attention to themselves by more distinctive calls, but because of the inexorable march of technology. Birdwatching – like everything else – has gone digital. In the old days (up to about 5 years ago!), a birdwatcher might carry a camera in the hope of grabbing what was known as a 'record shot' – distant, out of focus, lousy light, but perhaps just about decipherable enough for a search for a match in a field guide. Nowadays, not getting several such shots is almost unforgivable. Just about everyone carries a camera in their pocket almost all the time, if only on their phone. A 'real' camera is still slim and tiny, but allows you to zoom in to even more detail, even after a bird has flown. But you still need a helpful well-illustrated book – like this one!

Bill Oddie, 2012

BIRD TOPOGRAPHY

If the illustrations on this page remind you of something you might see on a wall chart at a medical school, don't panic! Bird topography is indeed the avian equivalent of human anatomy. Every area of feathers has an internationally agreed name. Some of the terms do sound rather scientific. However, learning them is not as difficult as it may seem at first. Many are pretty self-explanatory: for example the bill, legs, rump and crown. Others sound more baffling, but in fact bird feathering follows a logical pattern and the topographical terms reflect this. For instance, the pattern on a bird's wing is more or less the same whatever the species and – once you understand the language, as it were – the names make sense: primaries (the first set of flight feathers), secondaries (second), tertials (third).

It is worth trying to get to know at least the basic terms as this does make it a lot easier to write an accurate description or do a sketch of a bird you don't recognize. 'Red median coverts and white moustachial' is so much more specific than 'red somewhere on the wing and white on the throat'. So, next time a bird stays still long enough for you to study it, try comparing these diagrams with the feather areas on the real thing.

Having said all this, I have generally avoided the more daunting details in the descriptions in this book. Bird identification can be tricky and it is often a challenge – although a rather satisfying one – but, in fact, my first message is: above all, don't be put off. It is definitely not so difficult as it may at first appear. Honestly!

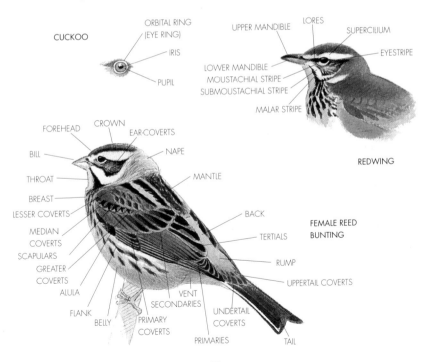

BEWICK'S SWAN *Cygnus columbianus*

122CM, 48IN

WHOOPER SWAN *Cygnus cygnus*

152CM, 60IN

Bewick's is the smaller of the wild swans. It is a winter visitor to Britain, and more numerous than Whooper, particularly in southerly areas. There are places where both species occur and give you a chance to compare them (try Welney). Bewick's has a slightly shorter and thicker neck, and the bill is neater and the area of yellow smaller and rounder compared with Whooper's. Juveniles are grey and the yellow on the bill is replaced by pink. On a reasonable view these differences can be spotted when the birds are flying. The calls are slightly different: Bewick's is a shorter, less echoing 'bugle'; Whooper's a little stronger and more eerie. Whooper Swan is about the same size as Mute Swan. Like Bewick's, it has a straight neck, yellow on the bill and a bugling call, and the juveniles are greyer, with pink bills. Compared with Bewick's, the shape of the yellow (or pink) is more pointed and extends further to the tip of the bill.

Bewick's Swan adult (right) and juvenile (below). As a general – but not infallible – rule, inland wild swans are most likely to be Bewick's.

Whooper Swan adult (left) and juvenile (above). Note extent of patterning on bill, extending further to tip, and shape of head compared with Bewick's. Whooper has a few regular wintering grounds, generally more northerly than Bewick's.

MUTE SWAN *Cygnus olor*

152CM, 60IN

The common British swan. Some individuals are barely wild and readily take food in parks and ponds; others prefer rather bleaker terrain on marshes and estuaries. The male (cob) has a larger bill knob than the female (pen). Juveniles start off grey and become whiter over the following couple of years. The bill also turns from grey to the adult black and orange. A swan is clearly a swan, unless seen at a distance asleep, in which case it could be mistaken for another large white bird such as a Spoonbill or egret. There are also a few white (ex-farmyard) geese around to confuse the issue. Distinguishing Mute Swan from the genuinely wild swans (Bewick's and Whooper) can be a little trickier. Mute usually holds its neck in a graceful curve; wild swans' necks are straight. One basic fact to remember: wild swans are only winter visitors to Britain, and they generally favour regular wintering grounds.

Mute Swan (far left), **Whooper Swan** (centre) and **Bewick's Swan** (near left). In flight, Mute Swans' wings 'whistle'. Wild swans' wings are silent, but the birds rarely are; if you see them flying, you'll probably hear them bugling too.

Mute Swan adult (below, left) and **juvenile**. Note black knob at base of adult's bill. Mute Swans are indeed mute (except for a few soft, wheezy noises).

GREYLAG GOOSE *Anser anser*

76–89CM, 30–35IN

The Greylag is the most widespread of British geese. Identifying the different species isn't easy. Calls are important. Greylags really do honk and squawk like their farmyard cousins. They belong to the group known as grey geese. The important areas to note are the colours of the legs and beaks, and any markings on the head, wings or belly. Greylags have large orange bills, pinkish legs and a very pale chalky area on the upper forewing. A good rule is to get to know the Greylag, then compare other grey geese with it. The species occurs all year round, but all the other species of grey geese are winter visitors, arriving in late September and October and leaving in March and April.

Many Greylags are not really wild birds, but originated on farms or in collections and have 'gone wild'. They occur anywhere from park lakes and gravel pits, to remote marshes.

PINK-FOOTED GOOSE *Anser brachyrhynchus*

61–76CM, 24–30IN

Occurs in large flocks on its favoured wintering grounds. The smallest and neatest of the grey geese, with a gentle expression, round head and short neck. The neck and head are darker than the body. This is similar to Bean Goose (see page 226), but Beans are noticeably larger. Pink-footed has pink on the bill, and also – of course – pink legs. The forewing is bluish-grey, but not as chalky as a Greylag's. The call is a ringing 'ung unk' and a higher pitched 'wink wink wink'. Most geese will sometimes fly in a 'V' formation – they are famous for it – but don't assume that any distant 'V' of large birds 'must' be geese. Large gulls do this, as do Cormorants and even Curlews.

In a flock of mixed grey geese, Pink-footed Geese are relatively easy to spot due to their small size, dark necks and heads, and faint pinkish tinge to their body colour.

WHITE-FRONTED GOOSE *Anser albifrons*

66–76CM, 25–30IN

Another goose that occurs in large wintering flocks. Two distinct races occur in Britain. Greenland White-fronted Geese winter in Ireland and Scotland; Russian birds visit Wales and southern England. The traditional sites are well known and the best places to see them. Greenland-race birds have orange bills and legs. Birds of the Russian race have pink bills and orange legs. The adults of both races have white foreheads (the 'front') and black belly markings. These markings are lacking on the juveniles, which are therefore more easily confused with other species. In fact, only juvenile Greenland White-fronted and Bean Geese share the same bill and leg colour. Bean has the darker neck, head and wings, and is much scarcer and more local, so the problem rarely arises. Also, fortunately, most geese occur in flocks where adults are also present. White-fronted Geese have a pale forewing and even paler line down the centre, but not as pale as either Pink-footed or Greylag Goose. The call is higher pitched than the calls of other grey geese, with a whinnying quality.

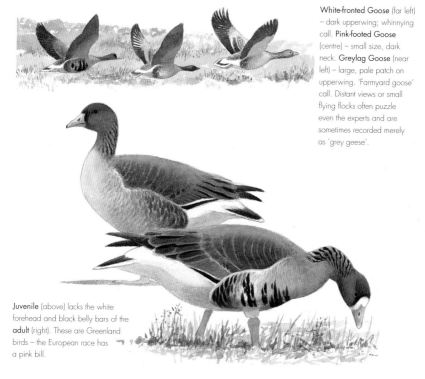

White-fronted Goose (far left) – dark upperwing; whinnying call. **Pink-footed Goose** (centre) – small size, dark neck. **Greylag Goose** (near left) – large, pale patch on upperwing. 'Farmyard goose' call. Distant views or small flying flocks often puzzle even the experts and are sometimes recorded merely as 'grey geese'.

Juvenile (above) lacks the white forehead and black belly bars of the **adult** (right). These are Greenland birds – the European race has a pink bill.

CANADA GOOSE *Branta canadensis*

92–103CM, 36–40IN

BARNACLE GOOSE *Branta leucopsis*

58–69CM, 23–27IN

The **Canada Goose** is the best known of the British geese, but is in fact native to North America. It is a common sight on just about any kind of water, particularly lakes and reservoirs, even in built-up areas. If you see a small skein of geese flying inland, it's not a bad rule to start by assuming they are Canadas. Canada's call is a loud honking, rather like an old-fashioned motor-car klaxon. Genuine wild **Barnacle Geese** are winter visitors in large numbers to a few favoured localities in Scotland and Ireland. Different populations breed in Greenland and Spitzbergen. On the wintering grounds, the flocks can be very large indeed – several thousand together. Smaller numbers may stop over at coastal locations in late autumn or spring, but very rarely in the south of Britain. A single goose inland is almost certainly an escape. Barnacle's call is very like the distant barking of a pack of small dogs.

Canada Goose. Large size, with chinstrap and brown body. Occurs all over the place, is present all year and breeds freely! Rarely flies as high as genuine wild geese.

Barnacle Goose. Smaller and cleaner black and white than Canada. White face, grey body. Only in winter at regular sites. Favours closely grazed grassland, but roosts on saltmarshes or mudflats.

BRENT GOOSE *Branta bernicla*

56–61CM, 22–24IN

The other British black goose (with Barnacle). Winter visitor. Very much a coastal bird of estuaries, marshes and farmland near the sea. A small goose, black and white like a Barnacle, but lacking the white face. Two races occur in Britain: Light-bellied on the west coast and in Ireland, and Dark-bellied in the east and south. They are becoming increasingly numerous in some of their favoured locations, and each year a very small number linger well into late spring or even summer. Brents are very rare away from the coast, though small parties do occasionally occur on inland waters, most likely on migration in late autumn or early spring. The call is a rather growly 'rronk', and a flock sounds as if the birds are conversing in somewhat guttural tones. Single birds inland are likely to be escapes.

Canada Goose (far left) – large, very rarely flies high, white chinstrap, honking call. Barnacle Goose (centre) – smallish, white face, barking call. Brent Goose (near left) – small, dark head, growling call. If you see a high-flying goose flock – even over town – that's the time to get excited! Look closely and listen for the calls.

Light-bellied Brent (left) and Dark-bellied Brent (above). A small, neat goose. Note Brent lacks the white face of Barnacle Goose. Feeds on coasts and estuaries.

SHELDUCK *Tadorna tadorna*

61CM, 24IN

A large duck with a goose-like shape and waddly walk. Present all year and breeds in the UK. Most common on the coast, on estuaries and marshes, but also occurs and even breeds inland, particularly at gravel pits or reservoirs with shingly or muddy banks. The plumage is very striking and almost unmistakable. Only the male Shoveler has similar colours – green head and orange flanks – but it is very different in shape and habits (see page 22). The male (sheldrake) has the larger red knob on its beak. Its calls are a rhythmic whistling and a short grunt. Young birds lack the orange breast band and red bill, and can look rather odd, but are not really confusable with anything else. Breeds in burrows and rabbit-holes, often in sand dunes, and leads a large party of dark brown and white ducklings after hatching. Several broods sometimes combine into creches. Adults gather in large flocks to moult after breeding. Gregarious, it is rarely seen singly.

Often whistles in flight.

Juvenile. Lacks the orange breast band and green face. Generally 'messier' than adult, but still the same, distinctive shape.

Female. Almost identical to male. This duck swims buoyantly, but rarely far out to sea.

Male. Larger knob on top of the bill than in female. Tends to feed by wading in shallow water and mud on the ebb-tide, sweeping for tiny snails in the soft mud.

MANDARIN DUCK *Aix galericulata*

43CM, 17IN

This is a bird that isn't a genuine wild species in Britain, but has now been accepted on the official list. A native of China, it was originally 'introduced' into ornamental wildfowl collections. There is now a small 'feral' (semi-wild) population, largely in the southern counties. Favours lakes – often quite small ones – surrounded by trees and overhanging foliage. Mandarins often sit on banks in the shade, and are very hard to spot, which is a pity, since the male is among the world's most beautiful birds. However, like all drakes, it can look less impressive when it is in moult during the summer and early autumn. Female and young Mandarins are very sombre: soft grey plumage, with a white chin and spectacle-like eye rings. Distinctive shape is clearly different from the shapes of other female ducks, and in any case due to its habitat preference it is rarely alongside any potential confusion species. Soft whistling call. Breeds in holes in trees.

Female (far left) and **male** (left). This species is in fact very rarely seen in flight. Flight call is a sharp whistle.

Female. Note the white spectacles. Confusable only with female Wood Duck – another wildfowl collection species (see page 224).

Male. Simply gorgeous in breeding plumage!

WIGEON *Anas penelope*

45CM, 18IN

Largely a winter visitor, occurring on reservoirs – particularly if they have grassy banks or farm fields nearby – and coastal marshes. Often seen in quite large flocks, feeding on pasture or mud, as well as swimming on the water. Male distinctive, with a chestnut head and cream crown stripe, contrasting with the pale pinky-grey body. In flight, white upper forewing patch is very obvious, and allows a flock to be identified even at considerable distance, for example flying over the sea in late autumn. Female is less dull than most female ducks, having a richer chestnut tinge and bluish bill. Note the slightly domed head shape, which is clearly different from the head shapes of other dabblers. In flight, female has a clean white belly, dark green speculum and pale forewing, making a distant flock distinctive. Eclipse males are like females, but still have white forewings. The call is a descending whistle that can be heard for some way: one of the most atmospheric sounds of winter marshes and estuaries.

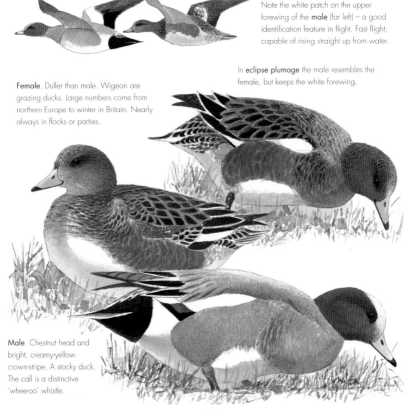

Note the white patch on the upper forewing of the **male** (far left) – a good identification feature in flight. Fast flight; capable of rising straight up from water.

In **eclipse plumage** the male resembles the female, but keeps the white forewing.

Female. Duller than male. Wigeon are grazing ducks. Large numbers come from northern Europe to winter in Britain. Nearly always in flocks or parties.

Male. Chestnut head and bright, creamy-yellow crown-stripe. A stocky duck. The call is a distinctive 'whee-oo' whistle.

16

PINTAIL *Anas acuta*

66CM, 26IN (DRAKE); 56CM, 22IN (DUCK)

Similar habitat preferences to Wigeon and – like that species – most common as a winter visitor to marshes and particularly estuaries, where it often feeds way out on the mud at low tide. The male is one of the most handsome ducks, with its black 'pin tail', chocolate head and gleaming white breast, which stands out a mile away even on the gloomiest winter days. The female, despite her inevitable browny plumage, has a very distinctive shape: slender slim neck, all-dark bill and a suggestion of the pin tail. A general note on the dabbling ducks: don't forget that all the males become like the females in eclipse plumage. Concentrate on the sizes and shapes – particularly the head shapes – speculum colour and upper forewing patterns. Also, don't forget that although each species has its preferred habitats, dabbling ducks can turn up on more or less any bit of water on migration or during hard weather, and they all occasionally fly over the sea, and even land on it.

Male (far left) and **female** (left). Female's slim neck and suggestion of pin tail stand out even in flight, along with a rather plain upperwing and dark dull speculum (the patch on the rear inner wing).

Female. Note distinctive shape (see text). Pintails are dabbling ducks like Mallard and Teal, and often occur with Wigeon, but their necks are longer and they have a more slender appearance.

Male. An extremely elegant duck. White breast often very conspicuous.

GADWALL *Anas strepera*

51CM, 20IN

Not a very numerous species, but seems to be increasing and is present throughout the year. Occurs mainly on inland waters and only very occasionally on coastal marshes or estuaries. Male is distinctive: soft grey with a black stern. Note the white speculum with chestnut and black edges. Female is very like a Mallard but just a little smaller. The white speculum is the best feature and is often visible even before the bird flaps its wing. A rare breeding bird, and even in winter doesn't often form large flocks. The white speculum allows identification of distant flying birds, but note that some of the diving ducks also show a similar marking, for example female Goldeneye (see page 23). A general note – although male ducks in eclipse are difficult to distinguish from the females, they retain the characteristic speculum colour.

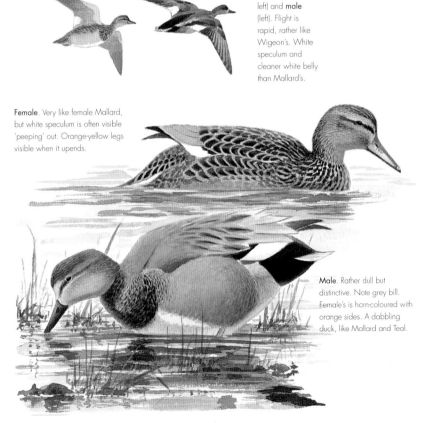

Female (far left) and **male** (left). Flight is rapid, rather like Wigeon's. White speculum and cleaner white belly than Mallard's.

Female. Very like female Mallard, but white speculum is often visible 'peeping' out. Orange-yellow legs visible when it upends.

Male. Rather dull but distinctive. Note grey bill. Female's is horn-coloured with orange sides. A dabbling duck, like Mallard and Teal.

18

MALLARD *Anas platyrhynchos*

58CM, 23IN

The common wild duck in Britain and many other parts of the world. Widespread breeder on all watery places from tiny ponds to coastal areas, sometimes even some way away from water. Male is familiar to most of us. Female is dull speckly brown, like many ducks. A good rule, though: get to know your female Mallard and compare other species with it. Note the head shape and size. Farmyard ducks are descended from the Mallard, and wild birds, especially in towns, often have patches of white in their plumage or may be pale in colour. The Mallard is a large duck, with a fairly large bill. Note also the purple speculum – the shiny patch on the wing. The call is the familiar quack. General note: ducks fall into a few convenient groups. On inland waters dabbling ducks feed by dipping their beaks beneath the surface or upending, and diving ducks do just that. They dive and swim under the water. Mallard is the archetypal dabbling duck, and the one to act as your basic comparison for all other ducks.

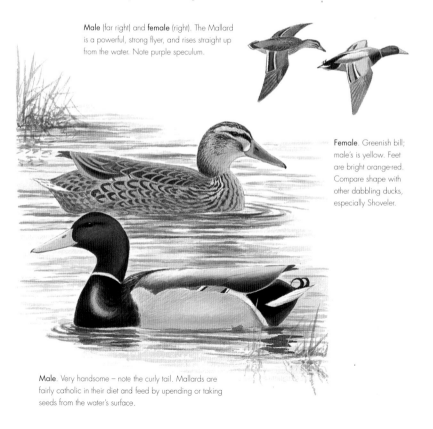

Male (far right) and **female** (right). The Mallard is a powerful, strong flyer, and rises straight up from the water. Note purple speculum.

Female. Greenish bill; male's is yellow. Feet are bright orange-red. Compare shape with other dabbling ducks, especially Shoveler.

Male. Very handsome – note the curly tail. Mallards are fairly catholic in their diet and feed by upending or taking seeds from the water's surface.

COMMON TEAL *Anas crecca*

35CM, 14IN

The smallest dabbling duck. Most likely to be seen in winter on large lakes – often hiding in cover at the edges – or on marshes and estuaries, where flocks may feed out in the open on the mud or on nearby grazing meadows. Always seems to be nervous and rarely allows close approach. Becomes even harder to see during the breeding season. Male is unmistakable: chestnut head with green eyepatch and striking creamy yellow undertail. The white flash along the side is conspicuous even at very long range. Female is a typical brown-mottled duck. Identify by small size and green speculum. Most similar to female Garganey (see opposite), Garganey has stripier face and is a summer visitor only. Call is an odd short 'peep peep', quite unlike a quack. Flocks of Common Teal fly very fast and low, and can be mistaken for waders at a distance over estuaries or marshes, or even over the sea during migration periods.

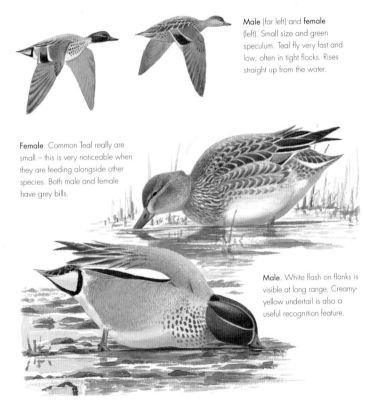

Male (far left) and **female** (left). Small size and green speculum. Teal fly very fast and low, often in tight flocks. Rises straight up from the water.

Female. Common Teal really are small – this is very noticeable when they are feeding alongside other species. Both male and female have grey bills.

Male. White flash on flanks is visible at long range. Creamy-yellow undertail is also a useful recognition feature.

GARGANEY *Anas querquedula*

38CM, 15IN

The summer teal. A dabbling duck that is a summer visitor to Britain, most commonly to the southern half of the country. It arrives in March and leaves by the end of September (rarely October). Usually seen in singles or pairs, and very occasionally small parties, but never in flocks like Common Teal. Much prefers secluded small lakes and fresh marshes, with reeds and ditches, and usually keeps to cover at the edges. The male is very distinctive, with a purplish head and vivid white eye brow, and shows pale blue shoulders when it flies. Female is very like a female Common Teal, but look for the paler stripes above and below the eye and paler forewing in flight. Flies fast but without the sharp twists and turns of Common Teal. Like all species of duck, juveniles – and males in eclipse plumage – resemble females, but the males retain a much paler forewing. Not particularly common.

Male (far left) and **female** (left). Compare with Common Teal. Note pale forewing – less bright on female, but still paler than in Common Teal. Flight is rapid, but not as wader-like as Common Teal's.

Female. Notice stripier face pattern than female Common Teal's.

Male. The vivid white eyebrow may be all you see when the bird is swimming among reeds and water-lilies.

SHOVELER *Anas clypeata*

51CM, 20IN

Like most of the British breeding ducks, a bird that is easiest to see in winter, when small flocks occur on inland waters and coastal wetlands. The male is very distinctive, with a green head, orange flanks and a bright white breast that is easily seen even at long distance. In flight, it has a bluish forewing. Female and juvenile: typically brown – like a Mallard or Common Teal – but note the obvious large bill and the distinctive feeding method: low in the water, dipping the head from side to side. Orange feet very conspicuous. Eclipse male can look a little like a Garganey, as it has a bluer caste to the head and whitish crescent in front of the eye, and bluish wing patches; but note the bill shape and larger size. Feeding flocks sometimes swim so close together it's hard to count them. Often, when food is plentiful, Shovelers seem to feed in cooperation, individual birds revolving slowly on their own axis in the water as they constantly nibble just beneath the water's surface.

Male (right) and **female** (far right). The blue forewing is the only colour on the otherwise drab female. Note the exceptionally large bill. Flies readily and well, but is a poor walker.

Female (left). Like other duck species, the female alone incubates the eggs. Shovelers usually nest on dry ground not far from water.

Eclipse male (right) in late summer/autumn. Shovelers tilt forwards to feed, swimming low in water. They do not upend as readily as other dabbling ducks, but can dive.

Male. The white breast is very conspicuous even at long distance. The huge bill is edged with a tiny fringe that filters seeds and other food from the water.

GOLDENEYE *Bucephala clangula*

46CM, 18IN

Diving duck. A winter visitor. One of the few species that is almost equally at home on the coast and on inland waters. Rarely occurs in large numbers – 50 in one place would be a lot – but is quite widespread. Just a few breed – in trees – mainly in remote parts of Scotland. Male: very conspicuous even at long range. Brilliant white and black (actually the head is dark glossy green, but often looks black). Female and juvenile: grey body, brown head. Young males look like females, but have more white in the wing.

In flight, the **male** (left) has very large white wing patch. **Female** (far left) has smaller white speculum on upperwing, similar to that in Velvet Scoter. The scoter is larger and darker.

Female. Slightly similar to brownhead Smew, but Goldeneye has wholly dark chocolate-brown head, and is confusable mainly because it keeps diving and gives only brief views.

Male. Note large head with noticeable peaked forehead. White face-spot conspicuous even from a distance.

A word on duck identification: males are generally pretty easy. Anything puzzling is likely to be a female or young bird. If the plumage doesn't quite fit the book it may well be a male in eclipse (moult), particularly in late summer and early autumn. Despite habitat preferences, birds can occur in the 'wrong' places (e.g. sea ducks inland, and inland ducks offshore). If you are really baffled: it might be a hybrid or an escape.

TUFTED DUCK *Aythya fuligula*

43CM, 17IN

The most common diving duck on inland waters, occurring in large winter flocks, but scarcer as a breeding bird. Often with Common Pochard. Male: clean black and white. Confusion only really possible with Scaup (see opposite), which rarely occurs inland. Note grey back of male Scaup, slightly larger size, and complete lack of crest or tuft on the head. Female Tufted compared with Common Pochard: darker brown, less grey plumage and rounder forehead, giving quite a different head shape. Many female Tufteds have a whitish area around the base of the bill, which makes them confusable with female Scaup. Female Scaup is larger, often has pale patches on the cheek, and the white area around the bill base is larger and clearer. Scaup really is a rare bird inland, and is also a winter visitor. Nevertheless, even experts often puzzle over blotchy female Tufteds. Also note that some female Tufteds have white under the tail and resemble the rare Ferruginous Duck (see page 225). Ferruginous has a pochard-shaped head, with steep forehead and generally more gingery tinge to the plumage.

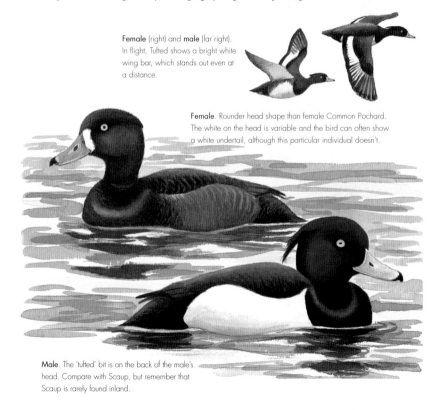

Female (right) and **male** (far right). In flight, Tufted shows a bright white wing bar, which stands out even at a distance.

Female. Rounder head shape than female Common Pochard. The white on the head is variable and the bird can often show a white undertail, although this particular individual doesn't.

Male. The 'tufted' bit is on the back of the male's head. Compare with Scaup, but remember that Scaup is rarely found inland.

24

SCAUP *Aythya marila*

48CM, 19IN

Mainly a winter visitor to Britain, and prefers the sea or inlets and estuaries, particularly in the north and in Scotland and Ireland. Often occurs in large flocks, which may extend into a long line of birds. It can occur on inland waters – especially in migration periods and during hard weather – but usually does so only in very small numbers. If you think you see a Scaup inland, look hard to make sure it isn't a Tufted Duck or hybrid. Male is very similar to Tufted Duck but with a grey (not black) back and no head crest. At a distance in poor light, Common Pochard can look similarly dark at both ends, but in fact its head is chestnut, and the head shape is different. Female Scaup is like a rather bulky female Tufted Duck, but with a larger, cleaner area of white at the base of the bill, often with pale blotches on the face, and a slightly sandier overall plumage tinge. In flight, Scaup also has a white wing bar, similar to Tufted Duck's.

Male (far left) and **female** (left).
Similar flight pattern to Tufted Duck.

Female. Note large white area at bill base and pale blotches on cheeks compared with female Tufted Duck.

Male. Note pale back compared with male Tufted Duck's.
Scaup are mainly sea ducks, feeding largely on molluscs.

25

COMMON POCHARD *Aythya ferina*

46CM, 18IN

One of the most common of the diving ducks. Present throughout the year. Large flocks occur in winter, although it is scarcer as a breeding species. Found almost exclusively on inland waters, from small lakes to huge reservoirs. May occur on rivers or even estuaries during hard weather. Male is distinctive: black at both ends and pale grey in the middle, with a striking orangey head. Female – as ever! – generally dull plumage. Often seen in company with Tufted Ducks. Female Common Pochard has a greyer caste than female Tufted, with paler areas on the face, including greyish spectacles. Note the pochard's characteristic head shape: steep sloping forehead. Tufted's head shape is rounder. In flight, Common Pochard has a rather uniform upperwing, lacking a vivid wing stripe. It tends to feed at night, so you are more likely to see it snoozing by day, with bill tucked back under a wing, often gathered together in rafts bobbing gently on the water. (See also Ferruginous Duck, page 225.)

Male (far left) and **female** (left). Diving ducks 'skitter' across the water's surface before taking off; when disturbed, they move out onto open water rather than take to the air.

Female. Greyer than female Tufted Duck. Note pale patch on face and 'spectacles'. Pochards usually dive for food – mostly plant material – but will upend.

Male. Note the typical posture – looks rounded. Distinctive head shape with sloping forehead. Often roosts on water by day.

COMMON EIDER *Somateria mollissima*

58CM, 23IN

A duck of the sea and rocky coastal areas, by far the most common in the north and in Scotland and Ireland, where it also breeds. Large flocks form in autumn and winter, which also consist of non-breeding birds. It is much scarcer in the south of Britain – most likely occurring offshore in autumn or winter – and very rare indeed on inland waters. Male is unmistakable in breeding plumage. However, young and eclipse males can look very blotchy and are very variable. Some look almost all dark, with a few white patches on the wings, whereas others have white breasts. Females are brown all over. Note the characteristic wedge-shaped head with long triangular bill. If you see any duck on the sea with this shape – even if the plumage is puzzling – it is probably a Common Eider. The only species that has a similar shape is Velvet Scoter, which is much rarer (see page 31). Call of male Common Eider is a surprised sounding cooing: 'oo oo oo'.

Male (far left) and female (left). The triangular head is noticeable even in flight. Strong, direct flight, usually low over water. Large numbers winter off British coasts.

Young males (right) often show this white-breasted look, but can have much messier patterns. The shape is distinctive. Adult male at foot of page.

Female (below). Note triangular head shape; this is a useful distinguishing feature from other female ducks.

LONG-TAILED DUCK *Clangula hyemalis*

DRAKE 53CM, 21IN; DUCK 41CM, 16IN

A sea duck, but one that prefers sheltered bays and estuaries. It also occurs occasionally – usually only in ones or twos – on inland waters, particularly gravel pits. A winter visitor. You are only likely to see large numbers in the north and in Scotland and the Northern Isles (Shetland and Orkney). The male's complicated black (actually dark brown) and white patterns are almost reversed from non-breeding to breeding plumage. The birds become darker as the spring progresses. Adult males have the wonderful long tail. Females and immatures are always duller than males, basically brownish above, white below, with white brown-blotched faces. The plumage is hard to describe, and in fact varies between individuals. Birds like this occurring inland are often a bit of a puzzle, somewhat resembling female Common Scoter or even Common Pochard. Long-tailed Duck is rare inland, so if you think you've got one, make sure to eliminate other confusion species. Dives continually. On sunny days, especially in spring, you may hear the cooing display call (like that of a small Common Eider).

Male (far left) and female (left). Unmarked, 'solid' dark wings contrast with the pale body and head plumage, making for a very distinctive pattern.

Male breeding plumage. Only likely in late spring in the north.

Non-breeding male. Arguably prettier than the breeding plumage.

Female. Young birds look basically like females but are variable and can be a bit of a puzzle (see text). Remember that Long-tailed is rare inland.

SMEW *Mergellus albellus*

41CM, 16IN

Winter visitor in small numbers to inland waters, particularly gravel pits. Also found on estuaries and inlets. Has a few favourite regular sites, and is more common in some winters than in others, particularly if it is cold on the Continent. The Smew is the smallest of the sawbills (which have serrated beaks for gripping fish). The male is exquisite – unmistakable – brilliant white, with black 'cracks' and eye patch. Female and juvenile are grey, with a chestnut crown and white cheeks. Female Common Scoter also has the white-cheeked look, but is different in shape and the crown is not chestnut. Brownhead Goldeneye, with which Smew often occurs, has similar habits – constantly diving – and basically similar colours, but lacks the white cheeks. Brownhead Smew are considerably more numerous than the lovely males in breeding plumage – a pity! A shy and almost silent bird, it flies fast and is an expert diver.

Female (right) and **male** (far right). Only likely to be seen 'skittering' across the water when disturbed. Adult male looks more pied in flight than when on water.

Female and **juvenile** are known as brownheads or redheads – arguably 'chestnut-head' would be most appropriate. Some other species have this white-faced look (see text).

Male. Small, neat and very pretty. Sadly, also pretty scarce in Britain, which provides wintering grounds for more female and juvenile birds.

COMMON SCOTER *Melanitta nigra*

48CM, 19IN

By far the most common of the two scoters. A sea duck that occurs in large flocks, mainly in winter, but also throughout the year in northern areas and Scotland. A rare breeder on a few remote Scottish and Irish lochs. Most likely to be seen on the sea or flying by on a seawatch. Also a surprisingly frequent visitor to large inland reservoirs, even sometimes during summer months. The male is all black, with yellow on the beak. Confusable only with Velvet Scoter (see opposite). Common has no white on the wing. Female Common is dark brown with a pale cheek that can look almost white. A female – especially on an inland reservoir – can be confused with female Smew or Red-crested Pochard, both of which have the pale-cheeked look. The Common Scoter is in fact considerably chunkier than all of them. In flight, Common Scoter males look all black and females more or less all brown: no wing markings on either.

Males are the only genuinely all-black duck in flight – but other species and distant flocks of ducks can look black in poor light or in silhouette.

Female. Several other species have this pale-faced look (see text and compare Smew and Red-crested Pochard).

Male. Only Velvet Scoter is as black, but Common has no white on face or wings.

VELVET SCOTER *Melanitta fusca*

56CM, 22IN

Occurs only very rarely inland. You are most likely to see it in winter with other sea ducks (especially Common Scoter) or flying past on a seawatch. In flight, both male and female show a bright white speculum on the upperwing, which immediately separates them from Common Scoter and Common Eider; but note that female Goldeneye also has a white speculum and may fly by on a seawatch. Female Goldeneye is smaller, with a paler body and chocolate-brown head – points are noticeable even in distant flight. Male Velvet Scoter is similar in shape and size to Common Eider, but has yellow on the beak and a small white patch under the eye, and is otherwise black. Female and juvenile are dark brown with whitish blotches on the face. The main problem with observing Velvet Scoters is often that they dive constantly, way out on rough seas, and it is hard to get a decent view, even with a telescope. It is always worth sorting through any flock of Common Scoters for the occasional Velvet.

In flight, both male and female look black or very dark, but with a vivid white speculum.

Female. 'Eider'-shaped head but sooty plumage. **Juvenile** looks very similar. Both male and female often show the white speculum even when swimming on the water.

Male. Only Common Scoter is as black. If white speculum is not visible, you may have to wait for Velvet to flap its wings.

RED-BREASTED MERGANSER *Mergus serrator*

58CM, 23IN

Present throughout the year, the Red-breasted Merganser is very similar to the Goosander (see opposite). Although mainly a winter visitor, it breeds in remote mountainous and moorland areas in small numbers, nesting on the ground. However, when not breeding it much prefers coastal habitats – bays and estuaries – where Goosander is much less likely. Smaller than Goosander. Male is much less 'clean' than Goosander, with a brown breast and greyer flanks. Brown breast band may also be a distinguishing feature in flight. Theoretically, male Red-breasted Mergansers have similar colours to a male Mallard, but confusion isn't very likely. Red-breasted Mergansers dive a lot and have a shaggy crest and scarlet saw-bill. Female and juvenile are very like Goosander, but note the wispier crest, less clear-cut white chin and overall scrawnier look, as well as a preference for salt water. Red-breasted Merganser is very rare inland. In flight, brownheads are even more similar to Goosander. Distant, constantly diving Red-breasted Mergansers can be mistaken for divers, Cormorants or Shags.

Female (right) and **male** (far right). Note large white patches on upperwing – much more than a mere speculum. Note brown breast band on male.

Female and **young birds** (left) are known as 'brownheads': compared with very similar Goosanders, they are more diffuse between brown head and whitish breast, and have a spikier crest.

Male (right). Wonderfully scruffy! Compare with clean-cut Goosander.

32

GOOSANDER *Mergus merganser*

66CM, 26IN

The largest sawbill. Mainly a winter visitor, but some breed in remote areas mainly in northern Britain. Like the Red-breasted Merganser, it feeds largely on fish; unlike mergansers, it nests in tree holes or among rocks. Mainly winters on large reservoirs, but also visits rivers and estuaries. Male: vivid white, with a dark green head (looks black at a distance) and scarlet bill. Female and juvenile: grey body, brown head, with a slight shaggy crest, very similar to brownhead Red-breasted Merganser (see opposite). Goosander has less crest, a cleaner white chin and slightly stockier build. Like other sawbills, patters along water's surface before getting airborne. Remember that Goosander is by far the more common species on inland waters; Red-breasted Mergansers prefer coastal areas. In flight, female Goosanders have a whitish broken speculum like Smew, but the patch is much larger. At a distance and in poor light, Goosander can be confused with divers, Cormorants or Shags, so look carefully at the shape and plumage colours.

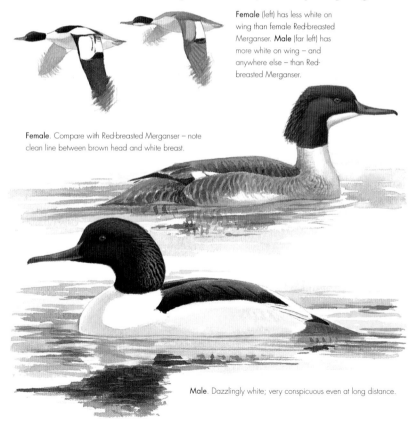

Female (left) has less white on wing than female Red-breasted Merganser. Male (far left) has more white on wing – and anywhere else – than Red-breasted Merganser.

Female. Compare with Red-breasted Merganser – note clean line between brown head and white breast.

Male. Dazzlingly white; very conspicuous even at long distance.

SIMILAR SPECIES: FEMALE DUCKS

All the species on this page are diving ducks. The habitat will often help identify them. Are they on the sea, a large stretch of inland water or a smaller reedy pool? On the opposite page are the female dabbling ducks, which do look very similar to each other – basically mottled brown. However, they all have their own distinctive shapes and plumage features, as well as characteristic ways of feeding and flying. Use the familiar Mallard for a reference point and comparison. Nearby male ducks will often enable you to work out what the females are, but the most difficult time of year is in late summer when most males are in eclipse plumage and resemble the females. Like marine species, ducks and other waterbirds can appear simply as silhouettes, so the more you know about jizz the better. Refer also to the main species pages for more information.

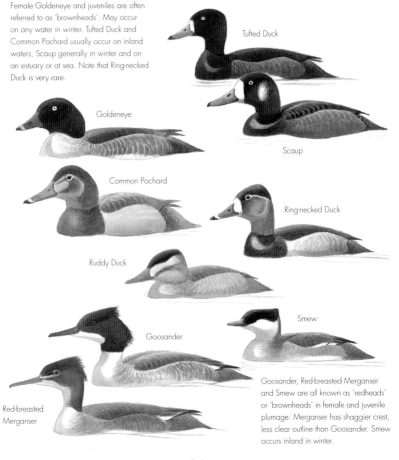

Female Goldeneye and juveniles are often referred to as 'brownheads'. May occur on any water in winter. Tufted Duck and Common Pochard usually occur on inland waters, Scaup generally in winter and on an estuary or at sea. Note that Ring-necked Duck is very rare.

Tufted Duck

Goldeneye

Scaup

Common Pochard

Ring-necked Duck

Ruddy Duck

Smew

Goosander

Red-breasted Merganser

Goosander, Red-breasted Merganser and Smew are all known as 'redheads' or 'brownheads' in female and juvenile plumage. Merganser has shaggier crest, less clear outline than Goosander. Smew occurs inland in winter.

Velvet Scoter, Common Scoter, Long-tailed Duck and
Common Eider occur mainly on the sea and are also diving
ducks. The other birds on this page are all dabblers.

Long-tailed Duck

Velvet Scoter

Common Scoter

Common Eider

Garganey

Wigeon

Common Teal

Pintail

Shoveler

Gadwall

Mallard

SIMILAR SPECIES: INLAND WATERS

Male Common Scoter

Male Long-tailed Duck

Female Common Scoter

Female Long-tailed Duck

Slavonian Grebe

Especially in autumn and winter, a large number of otherwise distinctive species can look rather drab. Many of them are basically dark grey above, with whitish faces. This page shows a selection for direct comparison. Compare, for example, Common Scoter with Ruddy Duck and Smew; Slavonian Grebe with juvenile Coot and Little Grebe; and juvenile Moorhen with Water Rail. As is the case with other groups, habitat preferences can be a useful guide – the Long-tailed Duck, for example, is rare inland.

'Brownhead' Smew

Female Ruddy Duck

Female Teal

Great Crested Grebe
(winter plumage)

Little Grebe
(winter plumage)

Juvenile Coot

Juvenile Moorhen

Water Rail

COMMON PHEASANT *Phasianus colchicus*

MALE 66–89CM, 30–35IN; FEMALE 53–63CM, 21–25IN

Found in woods, park and farmland in most parts of Britain. Many of the pheasants in Britain are hardly wild birds at all, since they have been bred and released purely to be shot and eaten. Pheasants never were true natives, since they were first introduced from the Far East back in Roman times. However, the plus side is that many pheasant woodlands also support other wildlife. In any event, a cock pheasant is a very handsome bird and pretty unmistakable. Female is basically sandy brown with darker speckles, clearly larger than a partridge and with a long, pointed tail. Pheasants do often interbreed with other more exotic races and species, and it is therefore not unusual to see a bird that has non-typical plumage. Some individuals are almost black, others lack the usual head markings, or have added patches of colour. Flight always looks a bit clumsy, with whirring wingbeats and a glide that threatens to turn into a crash landing! The male has a short, double crowing call: 'kor-kok'.

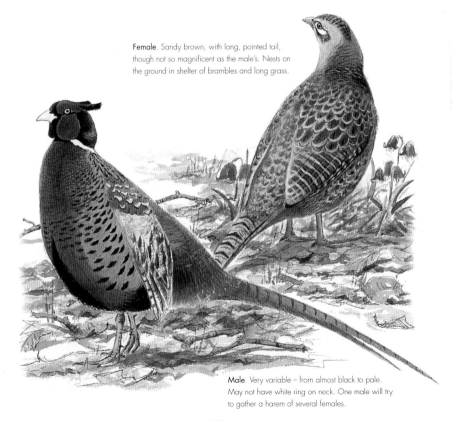

Female. Sandy brown, with long, pointed tail, though not so magnificent as the male's. Nests on the ground in shelter of brambles and long grass.

Male. Very variable – from almost black to pale. May not have white ring on neck. One male will try to gather a harem of several females.

37

PTARMIGAN *Lagopus muta*

35–36CM, 14IN

Found only on the mountain tops of central and northern Scotland. Most likely to be confused in summer with Red Grouse. Ptarmigan are slightly smaller, and always have white wings, which are usually visible even before the bird flies, if you can see it (they are beautifully camouflaged). In fact, if they are disturbed by people, they usually 'freeze', relying on their camouflage rather than flying away. In breeding plumage, the male is darker than the female and has a red comb above the eye. In winter the birds moult into almost completely white plumage, so that they blend into the snow. In autumn the males become greyer, and the white blotches begin to appear. Call is a short 'croak'; also a grating alarm call. Ptarmigans rarely come down from the mountain tops even in harsh winter weather. They feed on berries, seeds, plant shoots and leaves, and nest among heather and crowberry. The legs are feathered like those of Red Grouse.

Male winter plumage. Almost completely white, with a red comb over the eye. In breeding plumage it is darker than the female, but it starts to turn grey in autumn.

Female. When incubating eggs, the female relies on her exquisite camouflage for protection.

38

CAPERCAILLIE *Tetrao urogallus*

MALE 86CM, 34IN; FEMALE 62CM, 24IN

Found only in pine and conifer forests of central Scotland. Despite being a very large bird it is very hard to see, unless you happen to find a lek, where, early on spring mornings, the males display and sometimes fight for the attention of females. The male is as big as a large turkey, and overall largely blackish. It could only really be confused with male Black Grouse, which can occur in the same forests and also sometimes perches in trees, as does the Capercaille. Note that Capercaille really is much bigger and lacks the Black Grouse's white undertail and wing bar (though Capercaille does have a small white shoulder patch). Female Capercaillie is much smaller than the male but still slightly bigger than a grouse. Compared with Black Grouse female, she is paler, with a sandy patch on the breast, more obvious delicate barring on the upper parts and a rounded tail. Note, though, that young Capercaillies – like all game-bird chicks – can fly almost as soon as they are hatched.

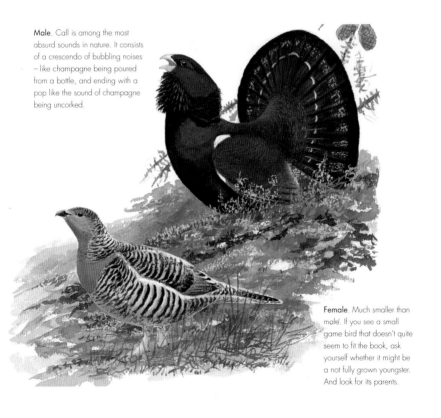

Male. Call is among the most absurd sounds in nature. It consists of a crescendo of bubbling noises – like champagne being poured from a bottle, and ending with a pop like the sound of champagne being uncorked.

Female. Much smaller than male. If you see a small game bird that doesn't quite seem to fit the book, ask yourself whether it might be a not fully grown youngster. And look for its parents.

RED GROUSE *Lagopus lagopus*

38–41CM, 15–16IN

Red Grouse are found only on open treeless moorland in the north and western parts of Britain and Ireland. Like all game birds, they are basically a bit chicken-like and if you flush them they fly away with whirring wings, often giving an alarm call. They occur in similar regions to Black Grouse and Ptarmigan, but as is the case with all game birds, the type of habitat often helps you identify them. Black Grouse are generally near to wooded areas; Ptarmigan occur only on the mountain tops of Scotland. Ptarmigan always show white wings. Red Grouse male and female are overall deep reddish-brown, with whitish underwings, which are quite conspicuous when they fly. The male is the redder of the two, and has a red comb above the eye. The alarm call is a cackling 'kowk kok kok'. Display call is often written as 'go back back back'. Grouse are larger than partridges (which rarely occur in the same kind of habitat anyway).

The usual view – flying away. If they've got any sense they won't fly this high on a shooting day! Flushed, they fly away on whirring wings. Underwings are whitish.

Male (right). Darker reddish-brown than female, with larger red comb.

Female (below). Very like female Black Grouse, but Black Grouse prefer to be close to wooded areas; Red Grouse are birds of open moorland.

BLACK GROUSE *Tetrao tetrix*

MALE 53CM, 21IN; FEMALE 41CM, 16IN

Slightly bigger than Red Grouse. Also lives on moor and heathland (but not in the south or east; absent from Ireland). Generally prefers to be closer to woodland or forest than Red Grouse. Conifers and birch woods are favoured. In late winter and early spring gathers at 'leks', where the blackcocks display to greyhens before mating. The males utter lovely cooing and bubbling calls. Males are very distinctive: black with lyre-shaped tails, and a gleaming white undertail shown off in the display. The hens are very similar to female Red Grouse, but are slightly larger and greyer, with a forked tail and a faint wing bar on the upperwing. Black Grouse occur in similar habitat to Capercaillie in the Scottish pinewoods and are not dissimilar. However, Capercaillie male is huge. The female is smaller but still bigger than a female Black Grouse and also paler and gingery, with more obvious barring (compare Capercaillie, page 39). Black Grouse sometimes visit grassy farmland to feed, particularly in winter.

Blackcock (left) – note double white wing bar.
Greyhen (above, right) – note faint wing bar on upperwing. Greyer than female Red Grouse.

Blackcock gather at a lek early in the morning in early spring. One male will mate with several females.

Blackcock displaying to a greyhen at a lek. When they aren't displaying they can be very hard to see – often lurking in thick forest.

41

RED-LEGGED PARTRIDGE *Alectoris rufa*

34CM, 13.5IN

There are two species of partridge in Britain: Red-legged and Grey. In flight, or seen scurrying through long vegetation, they can look very similar, but note that Red-legged Partridge is absent through most of western and northern Britain and does not occur in Ireland. It was originally introduced into Britain, and the further introduction of feral birds, plus the occurrence of the very similar Chukar Partridge, confuses the distribution, so it is best not to make assumptions. The two species favour similar farmland or open habitat – neither is likely on grouse moors – but they look very different when seen well. Note Red-legged's white face and black cheek edging (often the head is the only bit visible). The black neck and red-and-black flank stripes are also quite different from Grey Partridge's. The legs are indeed red (Grey's are yellowish). Red-legged Partridges are often seen in small groups and, when disturbed, they can run very fast as well as fly away. Call is 'chuck chukar', repeated.

If disturbed, Red-legged Partridges are just as likely to run as fly. Alarm call is a sharp 'kuk-kuk'.

Bright white face with black edging to cheeks, compared with sandy face of Grey Partridge, make it easy to distinguish from Grey, given a good view. Lacks dark belly patch of male Grey.

QUAIL *Coturnix coturnix*

18CM, 7IN

GREY PARTRIDGE *Perdix perdix*

30CM, 12IN

Quail is a summer visitor in small numbers, though in some years it is more numerous than in others. Most likely in southern Britain. Call: a distinctive 'quick kwi quick', sometimes written as 'wet my lips' (though I can't really hear that myself!). If you hear this sound in late spring or summer coming from deep in a cornfield or impenetrable vegetation, it signifies that a male Quail is in there somewhere. Your best chance of seeing it is simply to wait – it might just fly briefly. **Grey Partridge** is found in similar habitat to Red-legged. It seems to be declining in many parts of the country, where you are more likely to see Red-leggeds and Chukars. Usually best spotted by scanning across fields of short grass or crops. Even then, the birds tend to crouch low when feeding, or sit still when disturbed. In flight, they are not easy to separate from Red-legged. Call is a grating 'kerrr-ick'. The birds are often particularly noisy at dusk.

Quail (**male** in foreground with **female** behind). Likeliest confusion is with young game birds. Flight is very fast, whirring and usually short. If you are lucky the bird might scuttle across open ground.

A decent view reveals that **Grey Partridge** has a sandy – not white and black – face, and that the underparts are indeed grey. **Male** has a black 'horseshoe' belly patch.

Grey Partridge (**male**, far left; **female**, near left; much plainer **juvenile** behind). Favourite nesting site is under hedges or in thick fieldside verges.

RED-THROATED DIVER *Gavia stellata*

52–58CM, 21–23IN

Distinctive in breeding plumage in winter or juvenile plumage, divers are all basically black (actually grey) above and white below. At a distance Red-throated can be confused with Great Crested Grebe, Cormorant or Shag, or brownhead Goosander or Red-breasted Merganser. Breeds on isolated lochs in Scotland. In winter occurs on coasts around Britain, very occasionally on inland waters. At sea Red-throated is the most common diver; inland the rarest. The 'song' – only heard in breeding areas – is an eerie wailing.

Bill shape is key to identifying **non breeding-plumage** divers (below). Note upturned bill (noticeable even in flight) and white face, isolating the eye. In **breeding plumage** (top) red throat can look almost black.

BLACK-THROATED DIVER *Gavia arctica*

58–68CM, 23–27IN

Occurs around coasts (sea and estuaries) out of the breeding season, and also occasionally on inland waters. Less common than Red-throated on sea, but more frequent inland (though still a rare bird). Rare breeder on lochs, only in Scotland. Non-breeding and juvenile plumage is very similar to Red-throated's. Most similar to Great Northern Diver, but is slightly rounder-headed, bill is thinner and white flank patch is distinctive. Song – only heard in breeding areas – an eerie wail.

Non-breeding plumage. Note straight bill, slightly thinner than Great Northern's, and conspicuous white flank patch.

Breeding plumage. Very distinctive. Black-throated is almost the same size as Red-throated, but with a straight bill.

GREAT NORTHERN DIVER *Gavia immer*

68–81CM, 27–32IN

Breeding plumage rarely seen – this species doesn't breed in Britain – except in spring in the Northern Isles or on Scottish coasts. At other times, occurs on the sea and estuaries all around the UK and occasionally on inland waters (sometimes even quite small ones). Small, loose flocks may occur on coasts, but invariably solitary inland. In non-breeding plumage the same 'problems' as with the other two divers: i.e. confusable with Cormorants, and one another. Great Northern is the largest of the three divers. Note, in particular, the head shape: flat crown and square forehead. The bill is straight (unlike Red-throated's) and a little thicker than Black-throated's. It can appear quite pale, thus causing confusion with the very rare White-billed Diver. (White-billed has a slightly upturned look to the bill, which really is creamy white, including the upper edge.) In flight, the Great Northern's large feet are conspicuous, sticking out behind. A final word on divers: non-breeding birds are difficult, and even experts make mistakes!

Red-throated (left). Note the white face, visible eye and upturned bill. (Great Crested Grebe is smaller, with a longer neck, and more gangly in flight). **Black-throated** (centre). Black cap and invisible eye. **Great Northern** (right). Large feet are conspicuous in flight. Body is bulky.

Non-breeding plumage (below, top). The largest diver. Most similar to Black-throated, but note the flat head and thicker straight bill. **Breeding plumage** (below, bottom). Occasionally seen in spring, but does not breed in Britain. (Cormorants and Shags look heavier than divers in flight and swim lower in the water.)

FULMAR *Fulmarus glacialis*

47CM, 18.5IN

Widespread, breeding on cliff ledges in colonies, but most numerous in the north, Scotland and the Northern Isles. Feeds at sea, mostly on fish. Population has grown rapidly in the latter half of the 20th century. Superficially looks like a gull, but in fact belongs to the same family as albatrosses and shearwaters. At rest, grey above and white below, similar to many gulls, but note the distinctive 'tube nose' on top of the bill, characteristic of its family. In flight over the sea, could be confused with a gull, but notice the wings lack any black at their tips. Often runs across the water's surface to get airborne. Flies on very stiff wings, with much gliding, in typical shearwater style. It is, however, much greyer than any shearwater species, but – seen against the light – Fulmars can appear darker, and then confusion is possible. Good rule: if you think you are watching a shearwater gliding over the waves, are you sure it isn't a Fulmar?

The tube nose filters out salt from sea water. Don't approach a nesting Fulmar – it will spit at you and cover you in foul-smelling oil!

Grey plumage rather like a gull's, but note the lack of black wing tips. The flight is stiff-winged, with a lot of gliding. Never seen inland – unless it's been seriously storm-driven.

SIMILAR SPECIES: WINTER ON THE SEA

In winter plumage, many species become basically black above and white below, or – in cold wintery light – can simply look black at a distance. Shape, size and jizz become all important. In the labels for the illustrations below, 'M' stands for male, 'F' for female.

Great Crested Grebe
Red-necked Grebe
Slavonian Grebe
Black-necked Grebe
Common Scoter (F)
Common Eider (1st winter F)
Velvet Scoter (F)
Velvet Scoter (M)
Cormorant
Common Eider (M)
Common Eider (F)
Common Scoter (M)
Long-tailed Ducks
Great Northern Diver
Shag
Guillemot
Black-throated Diver
Razorbill
Red-throated Diver
Black-necked Grebe
Great Crested Grebe
Black Guillemot
Red-necked Grebe
Slavonian Grebe

MANX SHEARWATER *Puffinus puffinus*

35CM, 14IN

SOOTY SHEARWATER *Puffinus griseus*

41CM, 16IN

Manx Shearwater is the most numerous British shearwater, but still only commonly seen near breeding areas: e.g. Welsh coastal islands, some Northern and Western Isles and western Ireland. Unless you visit a colony at night with a torch, when the birds come to their burrows, you will only see shearwaters gliding low over the waves on stiff wings with intermittent flapping. Manxies are black above and clean white below. Possible confusions: Razorbills, guillemots and Puffins, but they flap frantically all the time. Good seasonal rule: shearwaters are very unlikely in winter. Spring and especially late summer and autumn are the best times to see them on a seawatch. Calls, at the burrows: unearthly, banshee-like grunts and wails. **Sooty Shearwater** is the second most common shearwater species in Britain, but is still a rare bird. Most likely to be seen offshore in late summer or autumn.

Manx Shearwater. Black above, white below, stiff-winged flight – the classic (and most common) shearwater.

Manx Shearwater. As its name implies, it glides low over the waves, well out to sea.

Sooty Shearwater. Note the silvery underwings, which flash as it banks and glides. Slightly larger than Manxie and not really confusable with that species.

Sooty Shearwater. It *is* sooty. Beware confusion with young Gannets, which are dark brown and do glide (Gannet is bigger and not such a fast flyer), dark-phase skuas and young gulls.

EUROPEAN STORM-PETREL *Hydrobates pelagicus*

15CM, 6IN

LEACH'S STORM-PETREL *Oceanodroma leucorhoa*

20CM, 8IN

European Storm-petrels breed on remote islands in burrows – where they only come in at night – mainly off Scotland and western Ireland. You are most likely to see them offshore in the breeding areas, probably following the wakes of boats. They will almost certainly be in a flock, possibly quite a big one. The only really likely confusion (apart from with some very rare storm-petrels) is with **Leach's Storm-petrel**. There are a few remote colonies in the Northern Isles off Scotland, but they are more or less unvisitable. Away from the nesting sites, it is in fact a rarer bird than European, but you are more likely to see one because Leach's are fairly regularly driven closer to shore – or even inland – by bad weather, particularly in late autumn. A rule: if you see storm-petrels over an estuary, or a single bird over a reservoir, they are almost certainly Leach's.

European Storm-petrel. May occasionally be driven close to land – maybe into a harbour – after very rough weather. Flight is fluttery and it hovers and drops onto the water when feeding.

European Storm-petrel. Tiny and fluttery, blacker than Leach's. Note white flash on underwing only. Never seen away from the sea.

Leach's Storm-petrel. Pale patches on upperwing and more buoyant tern-like flight. It lacks European's white underwing bar.

Leach's Storm-petrel. Slightly bigger than European, with longer, more pointed wings, a less clear white rump and a slightly forked tail.

SHAG *Phalacrocorax aristotelis*

76CM, 30IN

Basically the Cormorant's (see opposite) smaller cousin. The plumage is very similar except in full breeding dress, when the Shag has a quiff on its head, a greener sheen to the plumage, a yellow 'gape' and green eye, and lacks any white on the face or flanks. Juveniles are browner and paler below, and generally have the pale area more extensive than on Cormorant. However, plumages can look pretty similar, in which case size and shape are the key. Shag is quite a lot smaller (but this is hard to judge unless they are side by side – which they sometimes are). The head shape is different: Shag has a rather steep forehead, smaller head and thinner bill. Shags are very unusual inland, whereas Cormorants are common. On the coast, Shags tend to form larger flocks, but of course not always. Swimming, similar to Cormorant, low in the water, but head shape and size are still discernible. Final comment: it's no shame to puzzle over isolated birds; experts also make mistakes.

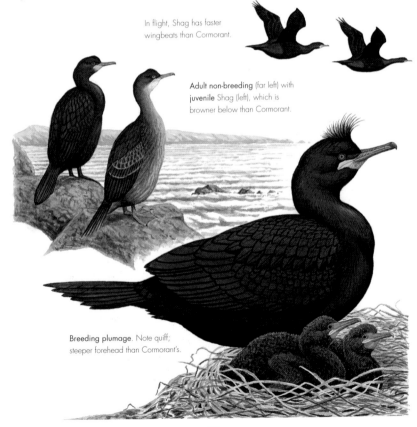

In flight, Shag has faster wingbeats than Cormorant.

Adult non-breeding (far left) with juvenile Shag (left), which is browner below than Cormorant.

Breeding plumage. Note quiff; steeper forehead than Cormorant's.

CORMORANT *Phalacrocorax carbo*

90CM, 36IN

Found all around the coasts, breeding on cliffs and islands, sometimes in small colonies. Also increasingly numerous inland on reservoirs, rivers and even quite small ponds. There are inland breeding colonies, usually in trees on islands on large lakes. May be seen perched high on trees, on rafts, boats and islands, where it often adopts its famous wing-drying pose. Adults are generally black, with a white dot on the flank in full breeding plumage, and some may have almost all white heads. Young birds are browner and can be quite pale underneath. Possible confusions: they swim and dive, and at a distance could be mistaken for divers (see pages 44–5). Flocks often travel in 'V' formation like geese. The only serious confusion is with Shag. Basic rule: inland, Cormorant is by far the most common; a large flock on the coast is as – or more – likely to be Shags. Cormorants are common coastally but rarely in such concentrated numbers. Shag is in fact smaller with a steeper forehead (see opposite).

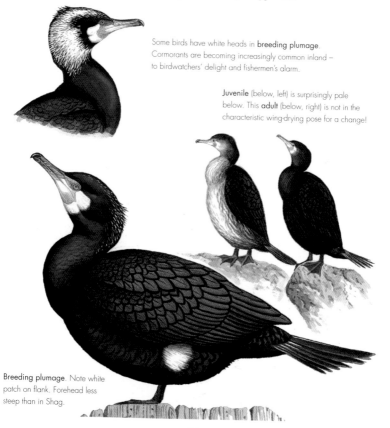

Some birds have white heads in **breeding plumage**. Cormorants are becoming increasingly common inland – to birdwatchers' delight and fishermen's alarm.

Juvenile (below, left) is surprisingly pale below. This **adult** (below, right) is not in the characteristic wing-drying pose for a change!

Breeding plumage. Note white patch on flank. Forehead less steep than in Shag.

51

GANNET *Morus bassanas*

90CM, 36IN

Breeds in colonies (often huge ones) on cliffs and islands, mainly in the north, and Scotland and the Northern Isles, with isolated colonies elsewhere. Adults on breeding grounds are unmistakable. Also occurs all around the coasts offshore among other seabirds. A line of Gannets is pretty distinctive, though they do bear some resemblance to a skein of geese (one of its other names is Solan Goose). Individual Gannets, however, can be quite puzzling, as they occur in a variety of plumages, from the almost black very young birds, to the pure white with black wing tips of adults. If they are gliding on stiff wings they can look very like shearwaters or even albatrosses (they have a 1.5m, or 5ft, wing span). If they soar high in the sky they may momentarily resemble skuas. Sitting on the water, they could even be mistaken for divers. So, a rule when seawatching: if you see a large, puzzling seabird, are you sure it's not a Gannet?

Gannets start life dark and get whiter as they get older. They take at least four years to mature. They can be confused with various other seabirds (see page 120–1).

Visit a Gannet colony for a noisy, smelly but unforgettable experience. They have a variety of interesting displays at the nest, and when out fishing are the most spectacular divers.

LITTLE EGRET *Egretta garzetta*

60CM, 24IN

A species that has been relentlessly moving north from its Mediterranean stronghold, its status changes every year. Certainly it is no longer a rarity, nor could it even be classed as 'localized'. Although the first British breeding records came, predictably, from near the south coasts of Britain and Ireland, colonies are now much more widespread. Little Egrets are generally tree or bush nesters, and the first pair to arrive in an area often latches on to the periphery of a (Grey) Heronry. You might think a gleaming white bird in the tree tops would be easy to see, but believe me when the canopy is in full leaf, it is very hard to spot. This is to a large extent because the birds really are 'little', and once they are standing or sitting on a nest they are totally hidden by twigs. It is a measure of Little Egrets' increase that there really are no patches of wetland – lakes, rivers, estuaries, marshes, reservoirs – where a sighting of a Little Egret would be a surprise. Forty years ago it would have attracted a 'twitch'. In breeding plumage, Little Egrets look delightful. However, they produce a guttural gargle that may strike you as comical or slightly revolting!

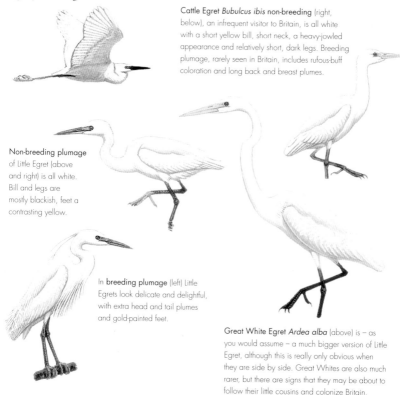

Cattle Egret *Bubulcus ibis* non-breeding (right, below), an infrequent visitor to Britain, is all white with a short yellow bill, short neck, a heavy-jowled appearance and relatively short, dark legs. Breeding plumage, rarely seen in Britain, includes rufous-buff coloration and long back and breast plumes.

Non-breeding plumage of Little Egret (above and right) is all white. Bill and legs are mostly blackish, feet a contrasting yellow.

In breeding plumage (left) Little Egrets look delicate and delightful, with extra head and tail plumes and gold-painted feet.

Great White Egret *Ardea alba* (above) is – as you would assume – a much bigger version of Little Egret, although this is really only obvious when they are side by side. Great Whites are also much rarer, but there are signs that they may be about to follow their little cousins and colonize Britain.

BITTERN *Botaurus stellaris*

75CM, 30IN

Sadly, a very rare bird, though numbers have risen recently due to conservation efforts. Scarce breeder deep in the reedbeds in East Anglia and a few other protected marshes. Even there, it is not often seen. Your best bet is if one flies, which they occasionally do, though usually not for long, soon dropping back down out of sight. In fact, Bitterns are so rarely seen in flight that they are often puzzling: I have known them to be mistaken for birds of prey, day-flying owls and the rare Purple Heron. If you are very lucky you may see one 'on the ground', most likely stalking through the reeds or posing absolutely still, either waiting for fish or relying on its camouflage. As well as the few breeding sites, there are a number of fairly regular wintering marshes, possibly frequented by continental rather than British birds. In fact, these are probably the best places to get a decent view, often from a hide. The call is an odd hollow 'boom' that sounds like a distant foghorn.

Flight is usually brief before the bird disappears back into cover.

You'll be lucky to see a Bittern out in the open like this. If alarmed, the bird freezes to merge into the reeds.

GREY HERON *Ardea cinerea*

90CM, 35IN

The common heron in Britain, and found all over the region. Occurs all year round in a variety of habitats: marshes, ponds, lakes, rivers, canals, estuaries and even rocky seashores. Hunts by stalking slowly through shallow water, or standing motionless and waiting for prey to come within reach. Usually nests in traditional colonies in trees. Juveniles lack some of the black neck markings of adults, but basically Grey Herons are pretty unmistakable. Nevertheless, they are sometimes reported as cranes. Cranes are in fact very rare and much bigger (see page 226), and they fly with outstretched necks (Grey Heron's neck is hunched). Flying Grey Herons are sometimes a puzzle, especially if they are soaring high in the sky over the middle of a city. Firstly, remember that they really are not uncommon in urban areas. Secondly, they do soar and circle and are often mobbed by small birds, which presumably mistake them for large birds of prey, as indeed do people! Call sounds like 'frarnk'; bill-clapping at nest.

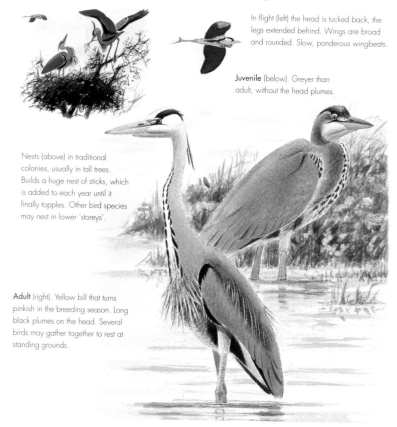

In flight (left) the head is tucked back, the legs extended behind. Wings are broad and rounded. Slow, ponderous wingbeats.

Juvenile (below). Greyer than adult, without the head plumes.

Nests (above) in traditional colonies, usually in tall trees. Builds a huge nest of sticks, which is added to each year until it finally topples. Other bird species may nest in lower 'storeys'.

Adult (right). Yellow bill that turns pinkish in the breeding season. Long black plumes on the head. Several birds may gather together to rest at standing grounds.

LITTLE GREBE *Tachybaptus ruficollis*

27CM, 10.5IN

Also known as Dabchick. Fairly common and widespread, found all year round on inland waters, sometimes quite small ones. In winter, small flocks can occur on reservoirs and estuaries, but very rarely on the sea. Breeding plumage is distinctive, with a rich chestnut neck and face, and a whitish puff-ball rear end. Youngsters are stripy and retain striped necks and heads for several weeks, even when fully grown. Non-breeding plumage is much duller, basically brownish above and whitish below, and the puff-ball look is often lost. This is when confusion is possible with the non-breeding rare small grebes: Slavonian and Black-necked. In fact, they are both much cleaner black and white. They are also much rarer, and generally prefer coastal waters. General rule: on inland water check that a distant small grebe isn't a Dabchick before considering the rarer ones. On estuaries and particularly on the sea, a small grebe is more likely to be a Slavonian or Black-necked. Song in the breeding season is a fast piping trill.

Juvenile (above, left). The stripes fade as it gets older. Tiny chicks are sometimes carried on the parents' back.
Non-breeding plumage (above). They don't always have this puff-ball look, especially if they have been diving.

Breeding plumage (below). Dabchicks don't often stay as still as this! They hide in reeds and dive a lot, staying underwater for about 15 seconds.

BLACK-NECKED GREBE *Podiceps nigricollis*

30CM, 12IN

A very rare breeding bird on just a few (usually secret or protected) inland waters such as lakes, large ponds and reservoirs, where it seeks cover in dense reedbeds or other vegetation. Picks insects off water's surface. Tends to be very shy in the breeding season. Moves to coasts in winter. Slightly smaller than Slavonian Grebe, which it closely resembles. Breeding plumage distinctive: note black neck and pale yellow 'ears'. Non-breeding plumage very similar to Slavonian Grebe's and the same possible confusions occur (see Slavonian and Little Grebes, page 58 and opposite). Note that the bill is slightly upturned (straight on Slavonian), the blackish cap smudges down below the eye (clean above the eye on Slavonian) and the white cheeks are more restricted (white almost meets on the back of the neck in Slavonian). Slightly domed top of head, compared with the flatter head of a Slavonian. The more common of the two rarer small grebes on inland waters. Slavonian is more common on the coasts, although neither species is very numerous.

Breeding plumage. The tuft of yellow feathers behind the eye is fan-shaped. Americans call this species Eared Grebe – 'golden-eared' would be more appropriate. A rare sight in Britain.

Non-breeding plumage. Very similar to Slavonian Grebe, but note the upturned bill, black cap smudging below the eye, and rounder head shape created by steep forehead and high crown.

SLAVONIAN GREBE *Podiceps auritus*

33CM, 13IN

Breeds only on a few lochs in Scotland. You are only likely to see breeding plumage there, on sea lochs or estuaries in spring. Non-breeding plumage is basically black above and white below. In winter (and autumn and early spring) may occur rarely on inland waters, and more commonly (but still not numerous) on estuaries or on the sea. Winter (non-breeding) plumage is very similar to Black-necked Grebe's. Note that Slavonian has a straight bill, the black cap does not smudge below the eye and the white cheeks almost join at the back of the neck. Both rare small grebes can be confused with winter-plumage Little Grebes, which can seem black and white, but are really shades of brown (see page 56). Also, young Coot are black and white, but only for a few weeks before they become all black. At a distance, some of the smaller female (or immature) ducks can look a bit like small grebes (especially if they are asleep). See female Smew.

Non-breeding plumage. Compare with Black-necked; note straight bill, 'clean' black cap through the eye and flatter head. Much more black and white than Little Grebe.

Breeding plumage. Definitely worth travelling to see. Note dark red neck and golden 'horns'. In fact, Americans call this species Horned Grebe. Note straight bill compared with upturned bill of Black-necked Grebe.

GREAT CRESTED GREBE *Podiceps cristatus*

48CM, 19IN

Widespread and common, the Great Crested Grebe breeds on inland waters, but is scarcer in the north. It makes a nest of weeds near the water's edge, hidden among vegetation. Breeding plumage unmistakable, with conspicuous ear tufts and ruff, known as a 'tippet'. Chicks start stripy and retain head and neck stripes long after they are full grown. Non-breeding (winter) plumage basically blackish (dark grey) above and white below. Confusion at a distance is possible with winter divers; also – especially when asleep – with brownhead Goosander or Red-breasted Merganser. On the other hand, the white breast is very distinctive even when seen at long distance. In winter occurs on coasts (estuaries and sea). Confusion is possible with Red-necked Grebe in non-breeding plumage. Rule: Red-necked is a rare bird (see page 60 for more). Great Crested Grebe flies with neck extended and drooping, giving it a hump-backed appearance. Call: harsh barking and chattering, especially when in courtship display, which involves graceful necking and the 'penguin dance', when both male and female almost seem to stand upright on the water.

Juvenile (at rear). Retains its neck stripes long after it is fully grown. **Non-breeding plumage.** Great Crested occurs on estuaries and on the sea in winter, so beware confusion with divers and other species.

Breeding plumage. Isn't it nice that such a spectacular bird is so common? The chicks leave the nest immediately after hatching and transfer to the mother's back.

RED-NECKED GREBE *Podiceps grisegena*

33CM, 13IN

A rare winter visitor, this species has tried to breed occasionally in Britain, especially in northern Scotland, but its attempts are usually unsuccessful and its locations are kept secret. Breeding plumage is distinctive – red neck, white cheeks, black crown, yellowish beak – but like all the grebes it becomes much duller in non-breeding plumage, when it is very much like the Great Crested Grebe, but slightly smaller. It occurs mainly in the winter months, rarely on inland waters, favouring gravel pits or lakes near the sea, or estuaries or offshore. Usually occurs as single birds. It is also seen on passage during the spring and autumn months. Distinguished from Great Crested Grebe by slightly smaller, shorter and stockier neck, and shorter bill, usually yellow-based. Duskier neck. Black cap down to the eye. Great Crested has white above the eye.

Breeding plumage. Unfortunately, this is a rare sight in Britain. Note the red neck, white cheeks and, compared with Great Crested, absence of head ornaments.

Non-breeding plumage. Most likely to be confused with non-breeding Great Crested (see text). Never forget: this species is much rarer, even at sea in winter.

RED KITE *Milvus milvus*

61CM, 24IN

A large, graceful raptor, with the looks of a harrier and the habits of a Common Buzzard! Genuinely British Red Kites are restricted to Wales, where the breeding population seems to be very healthy and slightly increasing. Scandinavian birds have also been introduced to English counties and are doing well. These may have noticeable wing tags on them. Red Kite has long, slim wings, a deeply forked tail and a foxy red tinge to the plumage, with whitish wing patches. At a distance, the forked tail may not be easy to see, in which case the flight style is the best feature to distinguish Red Kites from Common Buzzards, which are likely to be in the same area. Once seen, not easily forgotten! In the breeding season, Red Kites favour wooded valleys, where they can be very hard to spot, but there are several winter roosts – especially at 'feeding stations' – where up to a hundred birds can be seen together. Well worth a visit.

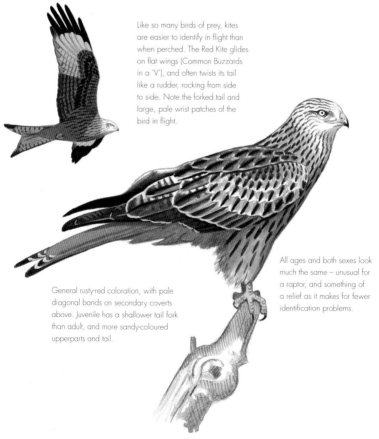

Like so many birds of prey, kites are easier to identify in flight than when perched. The Red Kite glides on flat wings (Common Buzzards in a 'V'), and often twists its tail like a rudder, rocking from side to side. Note the forked tail and large, pale wrist patches of the bird in flight.

All ages and both sexes look much the same – unusual for a raptor, and something of a relief as it makes for fewer identification problems.

General rusty-red coloration, with pale diagonal bands on secondary coverts above. Juvenile has a shallower tail fork than adult, and more sandy-coloured upperparts and tail.

61

MARSH HARRIER *Circus aeruginosus*

48–56CM, 19–22IN

Harriers are large birds of prey, as big as Common Buzzards, but with longer, narrower wings and longer tails, usually held closed. They typically fly low over reedbeds or farmland, with a flap and glide style, wings held in a shallow 'V', and frequently gently swaying from side to side, sometimes hovering and dropping onto invisible prey. Once seen, this flight style is not difficult to recognize. So, once you feel sure it is a harrier you are looking at, you have three species to choose from. Marsh Harrier is the most likely, though it is still not numerous and is restricted as a breeding bird to East Anglia. It is becoming more widespread, and prefers habitats that contain reedbeds or at least some wet areas. It is the bulkiest of the British species, noticeably a little heavier and broader winged in flight. Like other harriers, Marsh doesn't often soar up high and circle on the thermals. When it does, note the long, narrow-winged look compared with Common Buzzard.

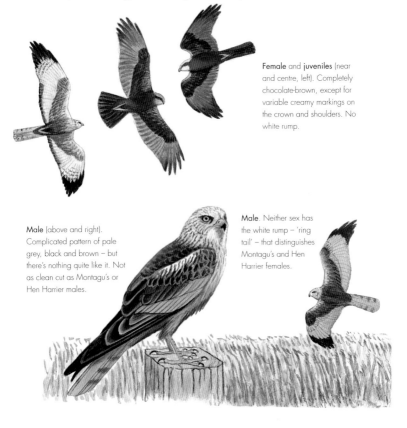

Female and **juveniles** (near and centre, left). Completely chocolate-brown, except for variable creamy markings on the crown and shoulders. No white rump.

Male (above and right). Complicated pattern of pale grey, black and brown – but there's nothing quite like it. Not as clean cut as Montagu's or Hen Harrier males.

Male. Neither sex has the white rump – 'ring tail' – that distinguishes Montagu's and Hen Harrier females.

HEN HARRIER *Circus cyaneus*

43–51CM, 17–20IN

Slightly smaller than Marsh Harrier (and Common Buzzard), with correspondingly slimmer build and narrower wings. The flight style is typically harrier-like (see Marsh) but Hen Harriers are less addicted to watery habitats. They breed (in small numbers) on treeless moorlands, particularly where there are grouse (which has made them the victim of illegal poisoning and shooting). The male is ghostly pale grey, with black, dipped-in-ink wing tips. It is even cleaner cut than male Montagu's Harrier (see page 64). Female and young birds are known as 'ringtails', because of the white upper tail band (rump), the only white area on the otherwise largely brown plumage. Ringtail Hen is extremely difficult to separate from Montagu's in similar plumage. It has a slightly heavier build, but this is hard to judge without experience. The really fine points of this tricky identification are covered in specialist books. Meanwhile, it's not a bad rule that birds seen in winter are almost certainly Hen Harriers, and especially if they are in a loose gathering at a roost.

Male (far left). Cleaner and more ghostly than male Montagu's Harrier. Also, its wing tips are black. **Female** on near left.

Male (left) and **female** (right). Female can be difficult to tell from female Montagu's, but note that Hen Harrier is the more common of the two.

63

MONTAGU'S HARRIER *Circus pygargus*

41–46CM, 16–18IN

Very like Hen Harrier, but a summer visitor only, arriving April and leaving by late September or early October. A scarce and decreasing breeder at a few well-protected sites, mainly in eastern England. Just a little slimmer and more graceful than Hen Harrier – sometimes likened to a large falcon – but it is hard to judge with a single bird. Males basically grey with black wing tips; also have thin dark lines running down the upperwing and light barring on the tail, and this makes them look less 'clean' than Hen Harrier. Ringtails are very similar to Hen, but the slimmer build may catch your eye, and the white rump may be narrower and therefore less vivid than in Hen. If seen well, perched – which isn't often in the case of harriers – almost or entirely unstreaked apricot-coloured breasts and bellies are visible in young Montagu's. Like Marsh Harrier, neither Hen nor Montagu's Harrier is often seen soaring, but this can and does happen, especially when the birds are migrating.

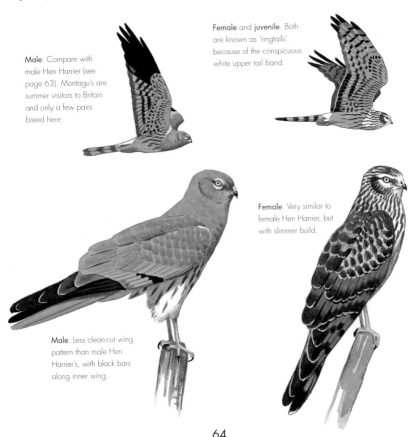

Male. Compare with male Hen Harrier (see page 63). Montagu's are summer visitors to Britain and only a few pairs breed here.

Female and **juvenile**. Both are known as 'ringtails' because of the conspicuous white upper tail band.

Female. Very similar to female Hen Harrier, but with slimmer build.

Male. Less clean-cut wing pattern than male Hen Harrier's, with black bars along inner wing.

SPARROWHAWK *Accipiter nisus*

28–38CM, 11–15IN

The second most common small raptor in Britain, often confused with the most common: the Kestrel. Sparrowhawks in fact belong to a different group – the accipiters – whereas Kestrel is a falcon. Falcons have slender, pointed wings, as does Kestrel, but Sparrowhawk's wing tips are more rounded. The flight style of a Sparrowhawk is quite distinctive: a shallow flap and glide that is hard to describe, but once seen is clearly different from a Kestrel's flight. Both species can soar and circle, in which case the wing shape is the best point to note, if you can't see plumage details (which is often the case with flying birds of prey). One perfectly safe rule, though: Sparrowhawks do *not* hover. They also generally hunt in wooded habitats, including gardens, where they glide low among foliage in pursuit of small birds. It used to be a fairly safe rule that any small raptor over a town would be a Kestrel, but Sparrowhawks are increasing and moving into urban areas. The most common call is a loud 'kek kek kek'.

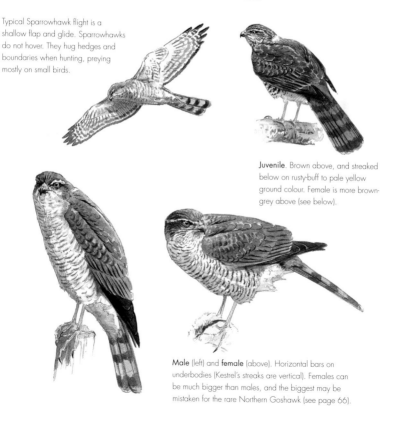

Typical Sparrowhawk flight is a shallow flap and glide. Sparrowhawks do not hover. They hug hedges and boundaries when hunting, preying mostly on small birds.

Juvenile. Brown above, and streaked below on rusty-buff to pale yellow ground colour. Female is more brown-grey above (see below).

Male (left) and female (above). Horizontal bars on underbodies (Kestrel's streaks are vertical). Females can be much bigger than males, and the biggest may be mistaken for the rare Northern Goshawk (see page 66).

65

NORTHERN GOSHAWK *Accipiter gentilis*

48–61CM, 19–24IN

Very much a large version of the Sparrowhawk. Two things to remember: Northern Goshawk is *very* much bigger – nearer the size of a Common Buzzard – and it is a much rarer and more secretive bird. Many claims of Northern Goshawk sightings turn out to be large female Sparrowhawks. Northern Goshawks breed deep in dense forests, where they are surprisingly elusive for such large birds. Like Sparrowhawks, they have a fast, low flight when hunting, but will take much larger prey, including rabbits. Courtship display flights can be spectacular. The plumage is much the same as Sparrowhawk's, but Northern Goshawk has a slightly hooded appearance to the head, and more obvious white undertail coverts. Neither of these points is easy to see, and the size and bulk of the bird – including a more bulging hind wing – are the best features. Juveniles have vertical streaking on the underparts, whereas those of young Sparrowhawks are horizontal like those of the parents.

Basically looks and flies like a large Sparrowhawk. However, note the bulging rear edge of the wing (secondaries) – straighter on Sparrowhawk.

Juvenile (below, left). Note underparts are vertically streaked (horizontal bars on Sparrowhawk).

Adult (above, right). Northern Goshawks are shy, elusive birds that live in deep forest. Never forget that they are much rarer than Sparrowhawks, and that female Sparrowhawks can be pretty big.

66

COMMON BUZZARD *Buteo buteo*

51–56CM, 20–22IN

The Common Buzzard is by far the most common large bird of prey in Britain, though not often seen in the east of England, but spreading even there. It is equally at home on mountains, moors and farmland, sometimes perching on posts right by the roadside, and is often seen soaring way up in the sky in wild country, where it is frequently mistaken for a Golden Eagle (see page 227). This only occurs in Scotland and the Western Isles (and a few individuals in the Lake District). A good rule is always to assume that a large bird of prey is a Common Buzzard until proved otherwise. Be aware, though, that other birds such as crows, gulls and even herons can soar up high in raptor-like fashion (see page 72). Note also that Common Buzzard's plumage is extremely variable. Some individuals can look almost white underneath, whilst others are very dark brown. There are all sorts of combinations in between. The paler forms usually have dark wing tips and 'wrists' on the underwings. The birds have a mewing call.

Adults (far left and centre); **juvenile** (near left). Birds of open country, Common Buzzards soar a great deal, often very high in the sky with wings held in a shallow 'V'.

Adult coloration is highly variable. May be whitish-buff and richly patterned below, or dark brown.

Juvenile is more streaked below than adult. Common Buzzards can often be seen sitting on posts adjacent to roadways. They feed mainly on small mammals, particularly rabbits, and also take a large amount of carrion.

OSPREY *Pandion haliaetus*

51–58CM, 20–23IN

A large raptor, as big as a Common Buzzard, but slimmer and longer-winged; not as slender as a harrier. Both male and female are dark brown above, almost silky white below, with a few darker markings on the underwing, and a striking white forehead with dark 'mask'. This is a non-variable plumage (makes a change for a large raptor!) and is very distinctive. Ospreys are dependent on water, since they feed on fish, which they catch in their talons. This is thus a pretty easy bird to identify. Not common, but the breeding population is healthy; the stronghold is Scotland, but 'introduced' birds breed successfully at Rutland Water in England, and no doubt more will follow. Summer visitor, arriving in late March or April, and departing by September or early October. At either end of this migration period, Ospreys may drop in to fish at almost any inland lake or reservoir. Call: like so many raptors a rather feeble noise, in this case a thin plaintive whistling.

The flight style is rather bow-winged, a little reminiscent of a large gull. Spectacular plunge dive, with feet held forwards to catch fish, often submerging completely.

Male, female and juvenile all look much the same. Breeding almost entirely restricted to Scotland, but winters in Africa, so may turn up at inland waters further south when migrating.

KESTREL *Falco tinnunculus*

34CM, 13.5IN

Undoubtedly the most common and widespread British bird of prey. The familiar motorway hawk, often seen hovering over the verges, and it breeds even in the middle of cities, where its prey is principally small birds such as House Sparrows rather than the mice and voles that make up the bulk of its diet in the countryside. Males have bluish heads and rufous backs, while females are generally browner and more barred, and youngsters even more so. The call is a fast 'keekeekeekeekeee', often delivered from the air when the birds are indulging in their shallow-wingbeat, fast-flapping display flights. Kestrels usually nest in holes and crevices – in trees, buildings or rocks (Sparrowhawks usually make a nest of twigs in a tree). Distinguished from Sparrowhawk by more pointed, falcon-shaped wings and habitual hovering when hunting, as well as very different plumage, if you get a good view. It is worth familiarizing yourself with the size and style of Kestrel, as this helps to identify the other less common British falcons.

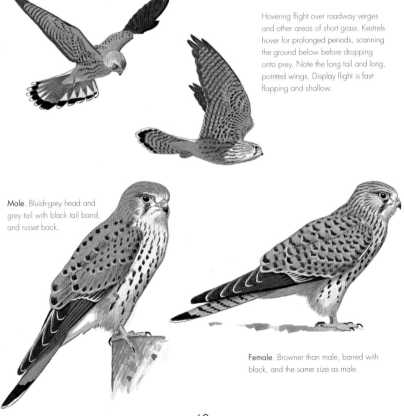

Hovering flight over roadway verges and other areas of short grass. Kestrels hover for prolonged periods, scanning the ground below before dropping onto prey. Note the long tail and long, pointed wings. Display flight is fast-flapping and shallow.

Male. Bluish-grey head and grey tail with black tail band, and russet back.

Female. Browner than male, barred with black, and the same size as male.

69

MERLIN *Falco columbarius*

27–33CM, 10.5–13IN

Merlins breed on wild treeless moorlands, and some of them descend to coastal marshes in the winter. Nowhere is this a common bird, and it tends to be elusive, often seen dashing away over the horizon. Your best chance of getting a decent view is of a bird resting on a post or rock at the coast between feeds, or if you happen to be close to a nest out on the moors (the nest is usually on the ground, among heather). The male is bluish-grey above, while female and young birds are brown. The most characteristic feature is its lack of moustaches, which all the other British falcons have to a varying degree. In fact, confusion is probably most likely with a young or female Sparrowhawk, which is also rather nondescript brown. Note the Merlin's more dashing flight style, and its preference for open habitat, where it feeds almost exclusively on small birds. You won't see a Merlin in a wood.

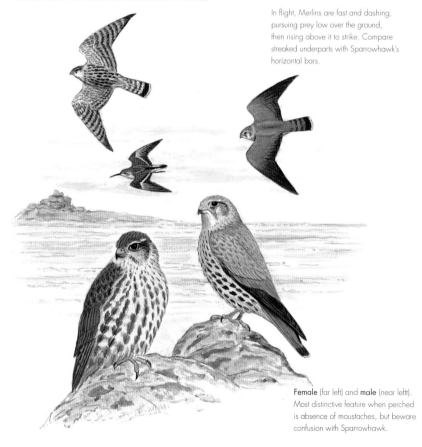

In flight, Merlins are fast and dashing, pursuing prey low over the ground, then rising above it to strike. Compare streaked underparts with Sparrowhawk's horizontal bars.

Female (far left) and **male** (near left). Most distinctive feature when perched is absence of moustaches, but beware confusion with Sparrowhawk.

PEREGRINE FALCON *Falco peregrinus*

38–48CM, 15–19IN

The largest of British falcons. Rather like a large, stocky version of Hobby, but more barrel-chested and with shorter wings. Peregrines are incredibly fast in the dive or stoop when hunting, but not as acrobatic as Hobbies. They are also all-year-round birds, breeding on cliffs and rock faces, but sometimes descending to coastal marshes during the winter. They are never seen in the same kind of wooded habitat as Hobbies. Their numbers are steadily increasing and they are now breeding on city buildings, as they do in parts of America. Male and female are bluish steely grey above, with horizontal bars on the underparts (Hobby's are vertical) and with very striking broad moustaches on a white cheek. The youngsters are browner and streakier. The call is the inevitable 'kee kee kee', but with a Peregrine's accent! Funnily enough, one of the possible confusion birds is feral pigeon, which can look surprisingly like a falcon (particularly Peregrine) when it is dashing away. Ironically, pigeons are among the Peregrine's favourite meals.

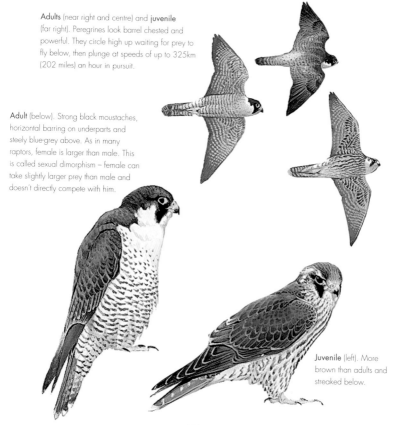

Adults (near right and centre) and **juvenile** (far right). Peregrines look barrel chested and powerful. They circle high up waiting for prey to fly below, then plunge at speeds of up to 325km (202 miles) an hour in pursuit.

Adult (below). Strong black moustaches, horizontal barring on underparts and steely blue-grey above. As in many raptors, female is larger than male. This is called sexual dimorphism – female can take slightly larger prey than male and doesn't directly compete with him.

Juvenile (left). More brown than adults and streaked below.

SIMILAR SPECIES: SOARING BIRDS

Birdwatchers – even experienced ones – sometimes make mistakes because they assume a distant bird (or flock of birds) is what they 'expect' it to be. Assumptions can be dangerous. Not all large circling birds are raptors; not all 'V' formation flocks are geese. A closer look through binoculars reveals the truth.

Soarers and circlers. These species are all capable of soaring way up in the sky in typical bird-of-prey fashion. It seems that even other birds are fooled, because they will often mob the raptor impersonator. Crows, in particular, seem to make mistakes (or maybe they just enjoy being belligerent!). Mind you, the frantic cawing of mobbing crows does often draw attention to a real raptor overhead.

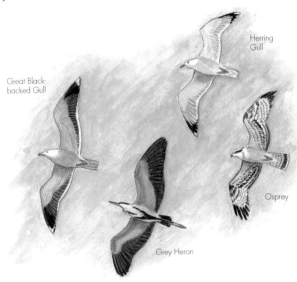

Large gulls, Grey Heron and Osprey: all may fly high and circle on thermals. Size at a distance is very difficult to judge, so you have to try to make out the bird's shape and any markings.

Herring Gull

Great Black-backed Gull

Osprey

Grey Heron

Common Buzzard

Carrion Crow

Crows can themselves soar and circle and look like raptors, but when you see one (or more) mobbing a Common Buzzard, you realize they really haven't got true raptor style.

Use your ears. Birds often call in flight. Common Buzzards have a distinctive mewing call.

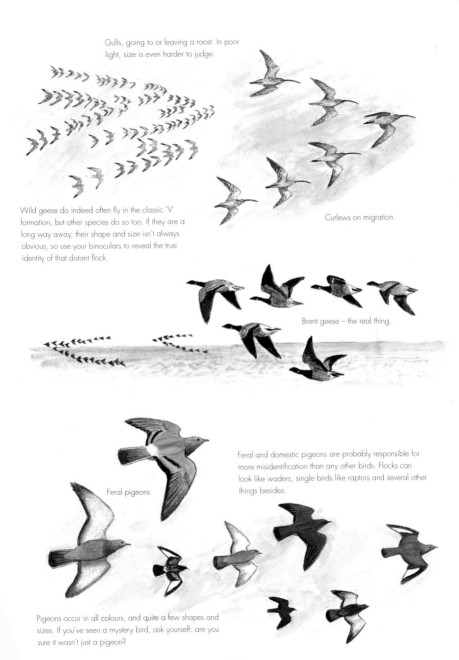

Gulls, going to or leaving a roost. In poor light, size is even harder to judge.

Wild geese do indeed often fly in the classic 'V' formation, but other species do so too. If they are a long way away, their shape and size isn't always obvious, so use your binoculars to reveal the true identity of that distant flock.

Curlews on migration.

Brent geese – the real thing.

Feral pigeons

Feral and domestic pigeons are probably responsible for more misidentification than any other birds. Flocks can look like waders, single birds like raptors and several other things besides.

Pigeons occur in all colours, and quite a few shapes and sizes. If you've seen a mystery bird, ask yourself: are you sure it wasn't just a pigeon?

HOBBY *Falco subbuteo*

30–36CM, 12–14IN

A summer visitor only. Arrives in April, gone by early October. Hobbies are about the same size as Kestrels and – if you can't see plumage details – then Kestrel is the most likely confusion species. Hobby has long, narrow wings, held in a slightly rakish, scythe-like position: often likened to the silhouette of a large swift. When hunting, it is very fast and acrobatic, sometimes suddenly changing direction as it zooms after large insects (dragonflies are a favourite and may be eaten while the bird is flying along) and sometimes small birds (particularly swallows and martins). Hobbies are fast! They rarely hover. They breed (not commonly) in woodlands, mainly in the southern half of England. Adult is deep bluish-black above, with clear moustaches, broadly streaked underparts and rufous leggings – all very different from a Kestrel. Juveniles are a browner version, without the strong colours or markings, but with the same fast shape and style. Call: 'keekeekeekee' (like so many small birds of prey). See also Peregrine Falcon (page 71), with which it could be confused.

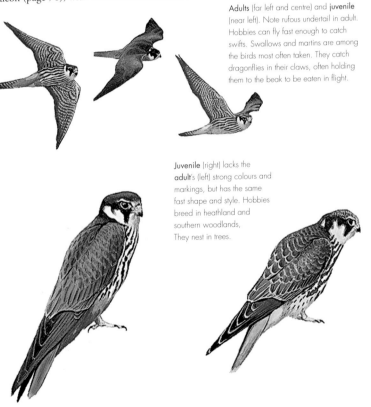

Adults (far left and centre) and **juvenile** (near left). Note rufous undertail in adult. Hobbies can fly fast enough to catch swifts. Swallows and martins are among the birds most often taken. They catch dragonflies in their claws, often holding them to the beak to be eaten in flight.

Juvenile (right) lacks the **adult's** (left) strong colours and markings, but has the same fast shape and style. Hobbies breed in heathland and southern woodlands, They nest in trees.

WATER RAIL *Rallus aquaticus*

28CM, 11IN

Breeds – very secretively – in marshy, reedy areas, and additional birds fly in from the Continent to winter in Britain. A bird that is probably more often heard than seen, and is perhaps far more common than we realize. It is very secretive in its habits, creeping around silently, either deep in reedbeds or in shady undergrowth in damp areas, sometimes even along woodland streams. Its call is a rather panicky wheezing or squealing – sometimes likened to a piglet in pain – or a sharp 'pip'. A sharp, sudden noise such as a distant gunshot – or even a hand clap – will sometimes provoke a call and betray the bird's presence. If you do see one, you will appreciate its general resemblance to a juvenile Moorhen, but note its smaller size, the long, thin red beak, greyer underparts and barred flanks. Young birds are more fawn coloured than adults, with a shorter beak, but they are very rarely seen.

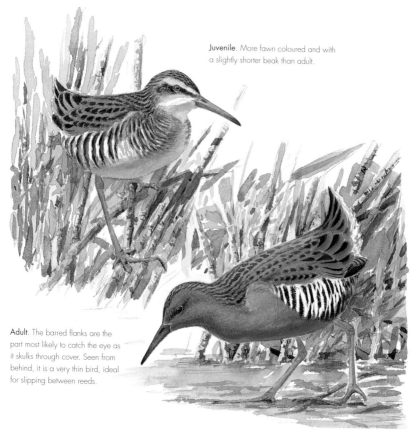

Juvenile. More fawn coloured and with a slightly shorter beak than adult.

Adult. The barred flanks are the part most likely to catch the eye as it skulks through cover. Seen from behind, it is a very thin bird, ideal for slipping between reeds.

MOORHEN *Gallinula chloropus*

33CM, 13IN

Widespread all over Britain in just about any damp habitat, including park lakes and ditches. Absent only from high moorland, fast-flowing rivers and saltmarshes. Although Moorhens are so familiar, non-birdwatchers seem to take time to sort them out from the almost equally common Coot. Adult Moorhens have a red-and-yellow beak, plus white areas on the flanks and tail, and although the rest of the body may look blackish, in fact it's a mix of dark blue and brown. Young Moorhens are the ones that can be a bit of a puzzle. They are simply brown and fawn, without any bright colours, and they are often skulky and merely seen scuttling into cover. Because of this they can be mistaken for Water Rails (see page 75) or even some of the really rare crakes (the family to which Moorhen belongs). Really tiny Moorhen chicks are all black (rather perversely, Coot chicks have red heads). Adults swim and walk with a jerky head movement and flicking tail. Call: a harsh 'krrek' or 'kittick'.

Juvenile (right). It's a good rule that if you think you may have seen a rare crake or rail, ask yourself if are you sure it wasn't just a juvenile Moorhen.

Adult. Common on ponds and rivers, often feeds on land. Swims with jerky head-nodding; unlike Coot, does not often dive, but capable of scooting underwater to avoid detection.

Moorhens (and Coots) are highly territorial, and fights among them are very common. They utter explosive 'kurr-ucks', 'kek's and 'kikik's during disputes, which can last many minutes.

COOT *Fulica atra*

38CM, 15IN

Almost as common and widespread as Moorhen, though there are parts of western Scotland where it is a scarce bird, and it generally prefers larger, more open water. Sometimes forms large flocks on lakes or reservoirs. Feeds largely on waterweeds, obtained by diving. Adults are black, with white beak and forehead shield (this is supposedly the 'bald' part!). Small chicks are black but with bald red heads for the first few weeks. They soon attain juvenile plumage, which is – rather surprisingly perhaps – white on the underparts. At this time, they can resemble winter-plumage small grebes (compare Slavonian and Black-necked Grebes, pages 58 and 57). The problem only occurs during a few autumn weeks, because Coot soon moult into adult all-black plumage. The most common Coot call supposedly sounds like its name: an echoey 'coot'. It also gives a sharp 'kik'. Coot can fly, sometimes going quite high and for a moment perhaps looking really puzzling, like some weird gangly duck with trailing feet.

Coot often gather in flocks, especially in winter. They prefer deeper, more open water than Moorhens, and dive to feed.

Juvenile (below). Has white underparts for a few weeks at the end of summer before moulting into adult plumage.

Adult (far right). White shield above white beak. At a distance, the rounded shape of the back is distinctive. Coot have feet with lobed webs on the toes. Moorhens have long, greenish-yellow toes.

Chicks (left). Tiny chicks are downy and wispy, with bald red heads. Adults are good parents, taking great care of their youngsters.

AVOCET *Recurvirostra avosetta*

43CM, 17IN

The symbol of the RSPB, largely because it represents a great conservation success. Avocets returned to breed in East Anglia after the Second World War. Now, thanks to the provision of carefully managed and protected bird reserves, their numbers are increasing and spreading. However, the breeding population is still mainly in the south-eastern half of England, at well-known sites. To breed and raise chicks successfully, Avocets need very precise conditions that will enable their invertebrate food to survive. Wintering flocks – sometimes of several hundred birds – gather at favoured estuaries in Essex and some southern counties. Wandering birds may occur further north or west, particularly during migration periods. A large, but supremely elegant wader, the Avocet's crisp black-and-white plumage and shape are distinctive and unmistakable. Younger birds have a browner caste to the back than adults. The call is a ringing 'kleep', rather more fluty than an Oystercatcher's. The extraordinary upturned bill is used to search for shrimps by sweeping with swift sideways flicks through shallow water and thin mud.

Dazzlingly white in flight. Often calls – a ringing 'kleep', rather more fluty than an Oystercatcher's.

Young bird (below). Less 'clean' on the back than adult. Very young chicks are speckled grey and have tiny upturned bills. The nest is a shallow depression on mud.

Adult (below). Avocets swim and upend like ducks as well as wade, and are found on estuaries, and salt and brackish marshes. Feeding involves brisk sideways sweeps of the bill.

OYSTERCATCHER *Haematopus ostralegus*

43CM, 17IN

Occurs all year round. Found all around the coasts, on sandy beaches and mudflats. Breeds in a shallow scrape on the ground in shingly areas, including on inland gravel pits, and has also moved inland to farmland, especially in some areas of Scotland, where it may be seen poking around on grassy meadows. In winter, huge numbers come to Britain, especially from Norway and Iceland. A large, conspicuous wading bird that really can't be confused with anything else. Lapwing and Avocet are also black and white, but quite different in shape and pattern and certainly don't have the Oystercatcher's carrot-coloured bill and pink legs. In flight, it shows a strong white wing bar, which again makes it easy to identify even at a distance. In winter it has a thin white collar. The call is a loud, piping 'kleep kleep', often uttered in flight, or in a display in pairs running together along the sand, bills pointed towards the ground. It feeds mostly on shellfish, especially cockles, which it hammers open with its powerful bill.

Easily recognized, the Oystercatcher is almost incapable of flying without calling noisily – a loud, piping 'kleep kleep'.

In winter Oystercatchers develop a thin white collar. Thousands come to winter on Britain's estuaries and coasts from northern Europe.

Male and **female** are identical. The long, bright red bill and pink legs make it easy to distinguish from other black-and-white birds, notably Avocet and Lapwing.

LITTLE RINGED PLOVER *Charadrius dubius*

15CM, 6IN

Very similar to Ringed Plover, and care should be taken when distinguishing the two. Ringed Plover is by far the most common. Little Ringed Plover is only a summer visitor, arriving in March and usually gone by the end of September. Little Ringed also prefers inland nesting sites – especially gravel workings – and even on migration is almost never seen on the actual coast (though it may occur on suitable habitat near the sea). The differences from Ringed are as follows. It is indeed slightly smaller – especially the head. Adults have a golden eye ring (not easy to see until you get close or use a telescope). Legs are duller straw colour, compared with adult Ringed's almost orange, and the bill is black compared with Ringed's orange with a black tip. Juveniles are similar to Ringed but retain the smaller head shape, have no white above the eye and have duller legs. The absolute fail-safe is when the birds fly: Little Ringed has no white wing bar, while Ringed does.

Adult. Even at an inland reservoir a mixed flock of small plovers on migration is likely to include more Ringed than Little Ringed.

In flight Little Ringed Plover has no wing bar and often calls – totally distinctive 'pee oo'. Compare with Ringed Plover (wing bar and calls a soft 'tooli').

Juvenile. Compared with Ringed Plover, smaller head shape, no white above the eye and duller leg colour. None of these points is easy to see at a distance.

RINGED PLOVER *Charadrius hiaticula*

19CM, 7.5IN

Ringed Plover is the most common of the small British plovers. It's a good idea to get to know it well, so that you can compare other species with it. It occurs all around the British coasts and also on inland waters with muddy or shingly shorelines, particularly during spring and autumn migration. It also breeds, mainly on shingle beaches, and sometimes on farmland near the coast, and rarely even inland. Call is a soft 'tooli'. The possible confusion species are Little Ringed Plover and the much rarer Kentish Plover. The first rule is to assume that any ringed-type plover is a Ringed, until proved otherwise. In addition, Little Ringed does not occur on beaches and mudflats, and it is also only a summer visitor. Kentish Plover is a rare non-breeding migrant, which occurs infrequently, mainly on south- or east-coast estuaries and beaches. It resembles juvenile Ringed Plover in having a broken breast band, but Kentish Plover has black legs. (For other differences see Kentish Plover, page 228.)

Adult. All plovers share the same basic shape: slightly dumpy bodied, relatively short-legged and short-billed, compared with other waders. Ringed can be used for comparison with others.

Juvenile. The breast band may even be 'broken' like Kentish Plover's, but note Ringed Plover's yellowish legs.

The simple distinction from Little Ringed Plover – note Ringed Plover has a wing bar.

81

GOLDEN PLOVER *Pluvialis apricaria*

28CM, 11IN

This and Grey Plover look similar but have very different habits. Golden Plovers breed on bleak moorlands, but winter in large flocks, usually on farmland or estuaries, often in company with Lapwings. In breeding plumage they are yellowish-brown above – 'golden' is a bit of an exaggeration – and black on the underparts. The northern race has more black than the southern. In winter, the black is replaced with whitish and the yellow upperparts become duller. Compare Grey Plover (opposite), which is not that dissimilar, though its upperparts are indeed grey, lacking yellow tones. Grey Plovers do not breed in Britain and occur only on coastal mudflats, and very rarely on inland waters during migration. They never occur in dense winter flocks like Golden Plovers. Identification problems only really arise with single birds. In fact, Golden Plovers very rarely are on their own. Golden Plover is more slender than Grey Plover. In flight its silvery white underwing is revealed – compare with Grey's black 'armpit'. Golden Plover's call is a fairly short 'floo ee'.

Non-breeding plumage. In certain lights it might look rather less yellow than this individual and be confusable with Grey Plover. Usually in flocks in winter on estuaries and farmland.

Juvenile. Fast in flight. Note white underwing.

Breeding plumage. Northern race birds, most of which breed north of Britain, have black extending up onto the throat and face. Breeds on upland moorland.

GREY PLOVER *Pluvialis squatarola*

28CM, 11IN

Does not breed in Britain, but some birds may spend the summer on British estuaries. Does not visit dry habitat like Golden Plover; almost invariably seen on mudflats, beaches and estuaries, though occasional strays can turn up on inland waters. Summer plumage is most likely to be seen in late spring, as birds migrate north to their Arctic breeding grounds, or early in the autumn when they are returning south. At this time, quite large numbers sometimes occur, but they rarely flock together except at a high-tide roost. Breeding and non-breeding plumages are not dissimilar to Golden Plover's, but at no time does Grey show yellow tinges, and in flight the black armpit is easy to see and diagnostic. Greys are also a little stockier and thicker necked than Golden. Call is a long, almost mournful whistle, 'flee oo eee', which carries a very long way and often draws attention to birds flying overhead. Juveniles have neater white spots on the upperparts than adults.

Adult breeding plumage. Americans call the species Black-bellied Plover (presumably it was named in summer!). Some birds spend the summer in Britain, but do not breed.

Juvenile. Note Grey Plover's black 'armpit' (axillaries) – very easy to see when it flies. Compare with Golden Plover.

Non-breeding plumage. This really is grey. Juveniles have neater white spots on the upperparts than adults. Not likely to be seen in flocks except at high-tide roosts.

83

DOTTEREL *Charadrius morinellus*

22CM, 8.5IN

A very attractive plover with distinctive habits. A summer visitor only. There are really only two circumstances in which you are likely to see Dotterels: on the tops of mountains in the Highlands of Scotland, where they breed, or if you are lucky enough to come across or hear of a small flock – called a 'trip' – on spring migration. There are certain sites in England where birds seem to stop off nearly every year, sometimes staying for a few days to feed in spring wheat fields. Odd birds may also occur on autumn migration – usually on stubble fields at coastal sites – but they are pretty rare. Dotterel is a medium-sized plover – bigger than Ringed but smaller than Lapwing – and superficially a little like winter-plumage Golden Plover. However, if at all well seen, it is distinctive: no other wader has the vivid white eyebrow – which is sometimes all you can see above the vegetation – or the white breast band and orange belly. Another wader that doesn't wade.

Juvenile. A sort of washed-out version of the adult, with all markings much fainter.

Note no wing bar in flight – most other plovers have one. Dotterel is a rare summer visitor, breeding on mountain tops in the Scottish Highlands.

Adult. The females are actually brighter than the males. Males do most of the incubating and caring for the young and therefore need to be less conspicuous on the nest.

LAPWING *Vanellus vanellus*

30CM, 12IN

The most common and therefore the most familiar of the larger British plovers. It is sometimes known as Green Plover because of its plumage, or Peewit after its call. It is a widespread but decreasing breeding bird on farmland, low moorland and the edges of large lakes. In winter, large flocks are a common sight on estuaries and coastal marshes, and during cold spells and snow they often undertake 'weather movements', when they may be seen flying high, even over the middles of cities, probably on their way to milder conditions in the West Country, Ireland or even Spain. On the breeding grounds, the males have a wonderful tumbling display flight, during which the wings make a humming noise that gives the bird its name. It's *not* 'flap wing', though to be honest that too would be appropriate, as the flight is indeed flappy. The winter flocks may be mixed with Golden Plovers, so it's always worth scanning through them.

Round wings and floppy wingbeats. Males in spring can be seen in tumbling display flight over fields.

The black-and-white plumage and round-winged, twinkly flight style makes a flock of Lapwings identifiable even at long distances.

Adult breeding plumage. At close range equally unmistakable. No other wader has the outrageous crest and glossy green plumage, though juveniles have a scalier look and shorter head plumes.

KNOT *Calidris canutus*

25CM, 10IN

Doesn't breed in Britain, but winters in large numbers: flocks sometimes comprise several thousand individuals. Knots begin to arrive in Britain in autumn and leave in spring, and may show tinges of breeding plumage, with a variable amount of red on the underparts. Confusion could occur with single birds or small groups looking a bit like Curlew Sandpipers or even Grey Phalarope. The latter is easily dismissed, since – as far as I know – Grey Phalarope has never occurred in Britain in full breeding plumage. Knot is clearly larger, shorter legged and straighter billed than Curlew Sandpiper. Winter- and juvenile-plumage Knot are basically grey above and white below. This is similar to other small waders, such as Dunlin, but again note that Knot is bigger, stockier and straighter billed. In flight, it also shows a pale rump, which Dunlin lack. Call is a rather subdued 'knut', rarely given or heard. A cloud of Knot veering over mudflats or coming into a roost is among the great wader spectacles in the world.

Adult breeding plumage. Any large flock, apart from in winter, may have birds showing variable amounts of red.

Juvenile. Like non-breeding plumage but neater upperparts feathers – seen only in autumn.

Non-breeding plumage. A typical grey-and-white wader, but slightly bigger and stockier than Dunlin and with a straighter bill. In flight it shows a pale rump.

SANDERLING *Calidris alba*

20CM, 8IN

Doesn't breed in Britain but is nevertheless a common sight on sandy beaches, where it – usually in a small, busy flock – chases the edge of the sea, as if playing tag with the waves. This behaviour is typical of Sanderling, and makes them easy to identify. However, occasionally, stray birds do occur away from beaches, even on inland reservoirs, and there they can be more of a puzzle. In late spring and early autumn, birds may be in total or partial breeding plumage, with scaly rufous upperparts and upper breast, and white below: not that different from some Dunlin or Little Stint. Sanderling is considerably larger than a Little Stint, and even a little bigger than a Dunlin. It is somewhat plump and short legged, with a rather short, straight bill. The call is a short 'pip pip', not unlike a Little Stint's, but quite different from a Dunlin's. In practice identification problems rarely arise, because Sanderling are far more likely to be seen on the beach chasing waves than mixing with other waders.

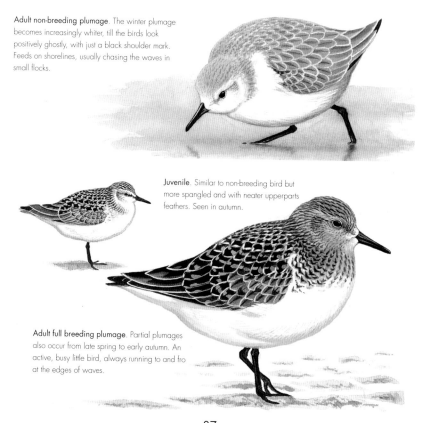

Adult non-breeding plumage. The winter plumage becomes increasingly whiter, till the birds look positively ghostly, with just a black shoulder mark. Feeds on shorelines, usually chasing the waves in small flocks.

Juvenile. Similar to non-breeding bird but more spangled and with neater upperparts feathers. Seen in autumn.

Adult full breeding plumage. Partial plumages also occur from late spring to early autumn. An active, busy little bird, always running to and fro at the edges of waves.

LITTLE STINT *Calidris minuta*

13CM, 5.25IN

Another small wader that is only a migrant in Britain. Scarce in spring, but more frequent in autumn. Often with Curlew Sandpipers and Dunlin, thus allowing direct comparison. Little Stint is clearly quite a bit smaller than Dunlin, with a shorter, straighter beak. It has a very busy feeding action, constantly picking at the mud. In breeding plumage the upperparts have a foxy tinge to them, which can extend onto the breast. In this plumage confusion could arise with breeding-plumage Sanderling, which just might occur at the same locations (compare Sanderling). But Sanderling are clearly larger, and generally prefer the seashore. Little Stints definitely prefer shallow, muddy wetlands and sheltered estuaries. Juvenile Little Stints, when seen close up and in good light, show an ochre tinge to the upperparts and a pair of white 'braces' down the back. Young Dunlin also have this feature, but rarely so cleanly, and again I stress that Little Stint really are little. The call is a rather feeble, short 'pip'.

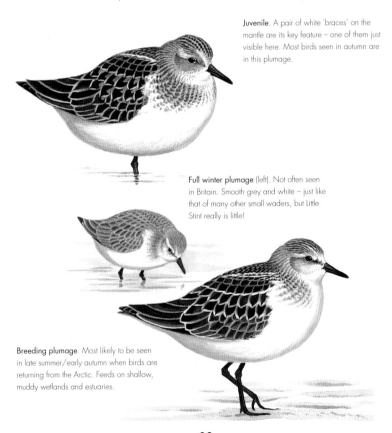

Juvenile. A pair of white 'braces' on the mantle are its key feature – one of them just visible here. Most birds seen in autumn are in this plumage.

Full winter plumage (left). Not often seen in Britain. Smooth grey and white – just like that of many other small waders, but Little Stint really is little!

Breeding plumage. Most likely to be seen in late summer/early autumn when birds are returning from the Arctic. Feeds on shallow, muddy wetlands and estuaries.

TEMMINCK'S STINT *Calidris temminckii*

14CM, 5.5IN

Temminck's Stint is a much rarer bird than Little Stint. A very few pairs breed in the wilds of Scotland, where it nests usually in sedge or marsh grasses. A small number of migrants passes through Britain each year, particularly in May, and again a few in August or September. Temmink's Stint prefers marshy freshwater habitat, and sometimes turns up on quite tiny wetlands inland, as well as near the coast. In spring, the upperparts are a similar colour to Little Stint's, though a little less reddish, and it has rounder feathers, giving a slightly smoother look. Autumn birds are much smoother, with a smudgy breast band that makes them look a little like tiny Common Sandpipers (see page 107), though it isn't confusable with that species. The simple way to separate Temmink's from Little is to look at the leg colour. Temmink's has relatively pale yellowy legs. Little Stint's are black. Temmink's has a soft trilling call (unlike Little's 'pip') and a characteristic towering flight. It is also generally a less busy feeder than Little.

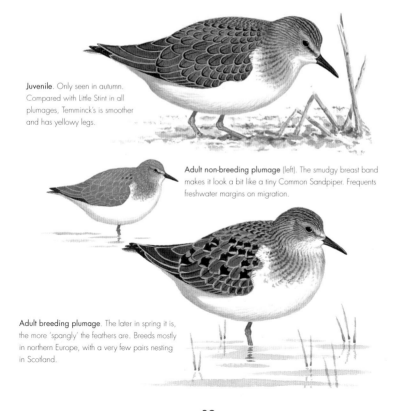

Juvenile. Only seen in autumn. Compared with Little Stint in all plumages, Temminck's is smoother and has yellowy legs.

Adult non-breeding plumage (left). The smudgy breast band makes it look a bit like a tiny Common Sandpiper. Frequents freshwater margins on migration.

Adult breeding plumage. The later in spring it is, the more 'spangly' the feathers are. Breeds mostly in northern Europe, with a very few pairs nesting in Scotland.

CURLEW SANDPIPER *Calidris ferruginea*

19CM, 7.5IN

The species that is probably most confused with Dunlin, since they are about the same size and share some other characteristics. First rule: Curlew Sandpipers are only migrants, which pass through Britain in spring and autumn, so don't expect them in winter. In May, late July or early August, they are likely to show at least some signs of breeding plumage, notably rich red patches on their underparts, different from Dunlin. The only other wader to show that colour is breeding-plumage Knot. This species is larger, shorter legged and straight billed (see page 86). Juvenile Curlew Sandpipers pass through Britain in late August and September. They are grey above and white below, and thus similar to juvenile or wintry Dunlin. Note the Curlew Sandpiper's slightly longer legs, smoothly decurved bill and softer grey back colour, with rounder feather shapes than a Dunlin and a gentle peachy wash on the breast. All these are subtle points. One feature is diagnostic: when the bird flies it shows a square white rump. The call is a soft 'churrup'.

A party could include an **adult in winter plumage** (near right) and **adult in partial breeding plumage** (far right), with different degrees of red on underparts and a few more variations in between.

Juvenile (left). Compare with Dunlin. It would be easier if it flew. Curlew Sandpipers have a white rump, and often share habitat with Dunlin, allowing direct comparison.

Adult full breeding plumage. Alas the least likely plumage to be seen in Britain, for Curlew Sandpiper is a passage migrant only.

DUNLIN *Calidris alpina*

17–19CM, 6.5–7.5IN

The most widespread small British wader. Knowing Dunlin is really the key to identifying similar other species. Small numbers breed on high moorlands, but you are far more likely to know them from coastal locations, inland reservoirs or sewage farms – both on migration and during the winter when large flocks occur. All plumages occur at these places. Breeding plumage is distinctive enough, with rufous upperparts and black belly. Juveniles lack the black. Winter plumage becomes basically grey above and white below, in common with many waders! Familiarize yourself with the size, shape, and bill and leg length of Dunlin – the overall jizz. Note that Dunlin has a fairly long bill, which is slightly kinked downwards at the tip. The call is a buzzy 'dzeee', which is hard to write down, but once heard is not difficult to recognize. As is the case with all waders, the call is very helpful to identification. It often clinches the species, so try to get to hear the calls and learn them.

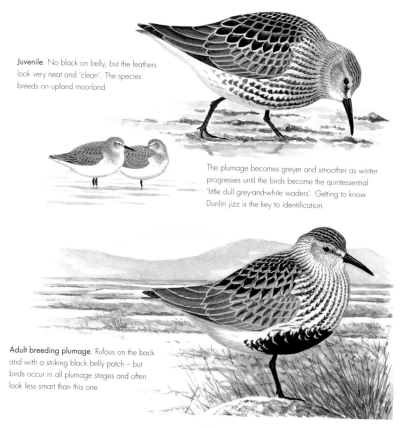

Juvenile. No black on belly, but the feathers look very neat and 'clean'. The species breeds on upland moorland.

The plumage becomes greyer and smoother as winter progresses until the birds become the quintessential 'little dull grey-and-white waders'. Getting to know Dunlin jizz is the key to identification.

Adult breeding plumage. Rufous on the back and with a striking black belly patch – but birds occur in all plumage stages and often look less smart than this one.

91

PURPLE SANDPIPER *Calidris maritima*

21CM, 8.25IN

A winter visitor with rather odd habits, which fortunately help to identify it. Purple Sandpipers only ever occur on rocky shorelines, or occasionally on jetties by the sea. They are absent in summer, breeding in the Arctic. Their plumage is hardly purple, more a sort of dark bluey grey. It is smoothest in mid-winter, becoming scalier as breeding dress appears. At all times they have yellow legs, which separate them from any possible confusion species. They are most similar to Dunlin, but are a little larger and clearly dumpier, though they too have a slightly decurved beak, which is yellow at the base. Purple Sandpipers are typically rather relaxed birds, often sleeping, which makes them very hard to spot among rocks and seaweed. They have a soft, chirruping call, which can hardly be heard above the noise of the waves. Very rarely, a Purple Sandpiper may stray to an inland reservoir, but if it does, it is almost certain to be on a rocky – or even concrete – shoreline.

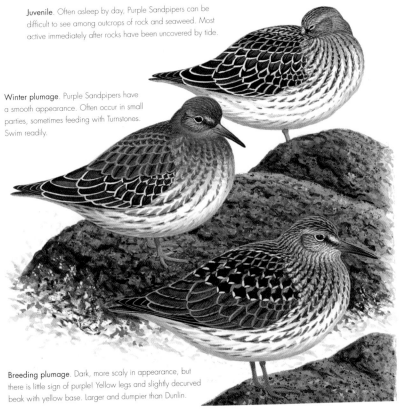

Juvenile. Often asleep by day, Purple Sandpipers can be difficult to see among outcrops of rock and seaweed. Most active immediately after rocks have been uncovered by tide.

Winter plumage. Purple Sandpipers have a smooth appearance. Often occur in small parties, sometimes feeding with Turnstones. Swim readily.

Breeding plumage. Dark, more scaly in appearance, but there is little sign of purple! Yellow legs and slightly decurved beak with yellow base. Larger and dumpier than Dunlin.

SIMILAR SPECIES: WINTER WADERS

A good approach if you see a wader you can't immediately identify is to eliminate the ones you know it isn't! Make a note of habitat – some waders prefer seashore, some open mudflats and others freshwater marshes. Also listen for calls.

Knot

Purple
Sandpiper

Little Stint

Ruff

Sanderling

Dunlin

Temminck's
Stint

Curlew
Sandpiper

Turnstone

In winter in particular many birds lose their distinctive plumage features and become basically grey – or brown – and white, so try to become aware of the differences in their shapes and sizes.

Black-tailed Godwits

Curlew

Common
Redshanks

Greenshank

Dunlin

Bar-tailed Godwits

Dunlin

Grey Plover

Common
Redshank

Knot

Sanderling

Little Stints

Dunlin

Ruff

Golden Plovers

RUFF *Philomachus pugnax*

29CM, 11.5IN (RUFF); 22CM, 8.5IN (REEVE)

Male Ruff in breeding plumage is one of the most striking birds. However, non-breeding birds can pose a real identification problem, especially as the females (reeves) are much smaller than males and look as if they ought to be a completely different species. If you are really puzzled by a small to medium-sized wader, ask yourself if it is a Ruff. First, notice the shape: a little pot-bellied with a rather slender neck, and a small head with a shortish, slightly downcurved bill. Then note markings, or rather the lack of them on the wings and rump. Wing bar is very faint. The rump is dark, but beneath is a sort of horseshoe-shaped white upper tail band. Sometimes this appears split, and sometimes it seems to join. There are several other waders that can look a bit like Ruffs – from Dunlin to Common Redshank to Wood Sandpipers – but none of them shows this combination of very faint wing bar and horseshoe tail band.

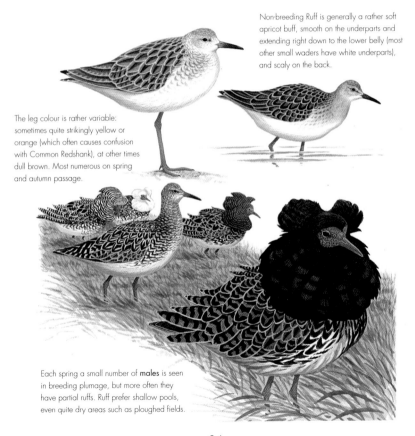

Non-breeding Ruff is generally a rather soft apricot buff, smooth on the underparts and extending right down to the lower belly (most other small waders have white underparts), and scaly on the back.

The leg colour is rather variable: sometimes quite strikingly yellow or orange (which often causes confusion with Common Redshank), at other times dull brown. Most numerous on spring and autumn passage.

Each spring a small number of **males** is seen in breeding plumage, but more often they have partial ruffs. Ruff prefer shallow pools, even quite dry areas such as ploughed fields.

WOODCOCK *Scolopax rusticola*

34CM, 13.5IN

As the name implies, Woodcock prefer habitats with trees. Your best chance of seeing them is at dawn or dusk, in spring and early summer, when the males make their regular display flights, known as 'roding'. To be honest, you will be very lucky to see Woodcock on the ground, as they like dark places and their camouflage is superb. They may momentarily look like owls. If you are lucky enough to get a close view, notice the cross barring on the dark crown, quite unlike a snipe's stripes. There is a certain amount of migrational movement around Britain, and birds also arrive from the Continent in autumn. At such times – particularly in October on the east coast – Woodcock may be flushed from relatively open habitat such as sand dunes or meadows by the sea, the same sort of places you may also see snipe. They will not utter the Common Snipe's distinctive harsh call, being either silent or maybe giving a soft grunt.

Breeds in some forested areas, particularly heathland with nearby conifers. Most likely to be seen at dusk or dawn, spring or early summer, in 'roding' display flight.

Surprisingly slow wingbeats – a bit owl-like – and makes soft clicking noises. Compared with Common Snipe, Woodcock is larger and has rounder wings and slower, straighter flight.

Larger and more barrel-chested than snipe, but with very similar plumage. Note cross-barred head. If disturbed, Woodcock dash away through the trees and soon disappear.

COMMON SNIPE *Gallinago gallinago*

27CM, 10.5IN

Common Snipe have a distinctive look and shape: very long, straight bill, very short legs and dark, heavily streaked plumage. Only Woodcock shares this look (see page 95). Generally, Common Snipe are rather secretive, feeding at the edges of marshy pools or in boggy ground. They breed on damp meadows, marshes and moorland all over Britain; larger numbers winter on lowland wet areas. They avoid the seashore. You are most likely to see them feeding out in the open on muddy pool edges in autumn. Otherwise, you more usually see them dashing away from you after being flushed. Call: a harsh 'scraarp', almost impossible to write down but once heard easily recognized. On the breeding grounds they have a wonderful towering display flight, producing a strange throbbing humming sound (drumming) by vibrating their outer tail feathers. They also have a high-pitched 'chip chip' call. Woodcock are larger and prefer dryer habitat. Jack Snipe are smaller winter visitors that are much rarer and even more secretive than Common Snipe (see opposite).

Common Snipe fly with a very fast zigzag style and almost invariably call: a harsh 'scraarp', difficult to describe, but once heard, easily recognized.

Common Snipe feed at the edges of marshy pools or in boggy ground, using their long bills to probe for worms.

To be honest, you don't often see Common Snipe posing like this – you're more likely to see them dashing away from you after being flushed.

JACK SNIPE *Lymnocryptes minimus*

19CM, 7.5IN

Common Snipe's rare little cousin, Jack Snipe are winter visitors to Britain. They appear in September and October and have usually left by April. They like the same kind of damp habitat as Common Snipe, but you are lucky to see one unless you literally almost tread on it. If you do see one in the open, it will usually be feeding along the edge of a marsh or sitting quietly almost hidden in the reeds. Seen well – compared with Common Snipe – note the more obvious double stripes on the head and along the back, shorter bill, the even squatter shape and feet that look a size too big for the body. Certain marshes seem to be favourite wintering places for Jack Snipe and may have small populations all winter – but in nothing like the numbers that Common Snipe occur. The only place you are likely to record more than one or two in a day are the Northern Isles (Shetland or Orkney) in October when migrants are arriving.

The escape flight is straight – not zigzagging like Common Snipe's – and usually low and short, before it drops back into cover and defies you to flush it again.

The feature most likely to attract your attention is its habit of bobbing on the spot, as if it were on a small spring. Jack Snipe are silent.

97

BLACK-TAILED GODWIT *Limosa limosa*

41CM, 16IN

There are two British species of godwit: Black-tailed and Bar-tailed. They are both large waders, near to the size of a Whimbrel, not quite so big as a Curlew. They share similar basic plumage: brown above and brick red below in breeding dress; brown above, whitish below in non-breeding plumage. They may occur together in similar habitats, mainly muddy estuaries and occasionally fresh water. By far the simplest way to tell them apart is to wait until they fly or preen, when they reveal their wing and tail markings. Black-tailed Godwit has a vivid broad white wing bar, white rump and broad black tail band. Bar-tailed has a plain brown upperwing, a less vivid white rump ('V' shaped) and – as the name implies – a barred tail (see opposite). Each year, a few pairs of Black-tailed Godwit breed in Britain in damp pastures, usually in east-coast counties. Their display flights are very conspicuous, with much loud calling and singing: 'reeka reeka, kweeit, weddy witoo', etc !

In flight – the easy way to identify godwits. Black-tailed has a vivid wing bar and a black tail.

Juvenile. A little less brick-red than adult. A few pairs breed in Britain in the eastern counties, on flood meadows and wet grassland.

Adult breeding plumage. Long-legged and long-billed. More graceful jizz than the rather 'squat' Bar-tailed. At rest the two species are less easy to separate, but there is a noticeable difference.

Non-breeding plumage. Compared with Bar-tailed, note smoother feathering on upperparts. Wintering flocks are largest in the west and in Ireland, involving birds from Greenland.

BAR-TAILED GODWIT *Limosa lapponica*

38CM, 15IN

Basically similar in looks and habits to Black-tailed. Does not breed in Britain, but large numbers winter there. The plumages are similar to those of Black-tailed, but the species are easily told apart when the wing and tail patterns can be seen – Bar-tailed has a plain upperwing and barred tail. In flight, the Bar-tailed's pattern is more similar to a Curlew or Whimbrel, but both have down-curved beaks and quite different calls. In flocks, especially on migration, Bar-tailed often gives slightly yapping 'kirrick' calls. If birds are feeding and hiding their characteristic wing and tail markings, they can still be separated from Black-tailed Godwit by their different shape: Bar-tailed is quite squat looking, with shorter legs and a slightly upturned bill. Also, note the back feathers are rather coarse and more pointed (like a Curlew's), compared with the softer, smoother look of Black-tailed. Although Bar-taileds generally favour estuaries and seashores, flocks on spring migration are often seen arriving over the south coast and carrying on inland. Occasionally they are spotted heading north, even over cities.

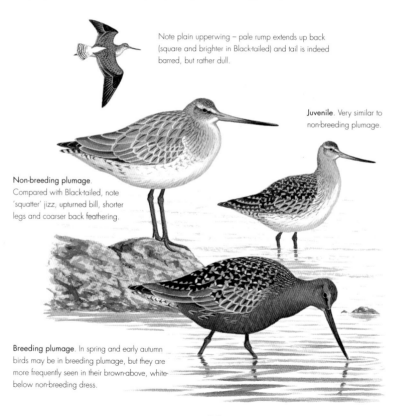

Note plain upperwing – pale rump extends up back (square and brighter in Black-tailed) and tail is indeed barred, but rather dull.

Juvenile. Very similar to non-breeding plumage.

Non-breeding plumage. Compared with Black-tailed, note 'squatter' jizz, upturned bill, shorter legs and coarser back feathering.

Breeding plumage. In spring and early autumn birds may be in breeding plumage, but they are more frequently seen in their brown-above, white-below non-breeding dress.

WHIMBREL *Numenius phaeopus*

41CM, 16IN

A summer visitor to Britain; small numbers breed on moorland in Scotland and the Northern Isles (especially Shetland). On passage, in spring and autumn, it is quite a frequent visitor to estuaries and coastal marshes, and occasionally inland. A few individuals stay all summer, and odd ones very occasionally winter. The plumage is very similar to Curlew's, but note smaller size, shorter, less decurved bill and pale stripe on a dark crown. Unfortunately, none of these features may be immediately obvious if the bird is flying. Listen for the call, a staccato high-pitched whistle, given as many as seven times in rapid succession – 'whi whi whi', etc. One of its local names is the Seven Whistler (though it doesn't necessarily utter seven calls!). Its call is quite different from Curlew's call (but just to confuse matters, Whimbrel do occasionally utter a 'curlew' call as well). Flight pattern is similar to Bar-tailed Godwit's and – since the species are about the same size – try to see the decurved bill on flying birds.

Note shorter bill, smaller size than that of Curlew, and a quite different call. Similar flight pattern to Bar-tailed Godwit's, so try to see the bill.

Note the crown stripes, which distinguish it from Curlew. If only they were always so easy to see! Mostly a passage migrant to coasts and estuaries.

CURLEW *Numenius arquata*

53–58CM, 21–23IN

The largest British wader. Large size, long, down-curved bill and unchanging plumage – always streaky brown above and white below – make this a familiar and easily identified bird. It even calls its own name. Breeds on moorlands and damp pastures in many parts of Britain, where it nests on the ground in a hollow among the grass. Larger numbers winter on estuaries, saltmarshes and farmland. Rather uncommon on inland waters on passage. On the breeding grounds, also has a wonderful bubbling song, delivered during the display flight, which is curiously fluttery and dainty for such a big bird. The most obvious confusion species is its small cousin the Whimbrel (see opposite), which is a summer visitor only (very rare indeed in winter), smaller, shorter billed and with stripes on a dark crown. The calls are quite different, and fortunately both species almost invariably do call a lot. A flock of Curlews on migration often flies in 'V' formation and could be mistaken for distant geese or large gulls (see page 120).

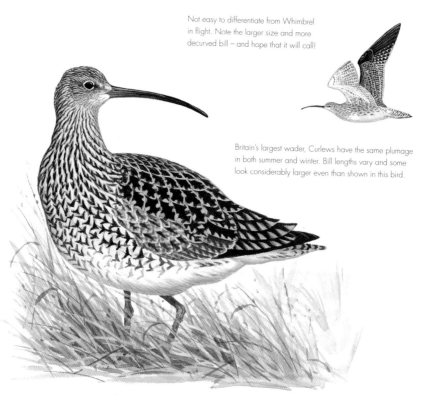

Not easy to differentiate from Whimbrel in flight. Note the larger size and more decurved bill – and hope that it will call!

Britain's largest wader, Curlews have the same plumage in both summer and winter. Bill lengths vary and some look considerably larger even than shown in this bird.

COMMON REDSHANK *Tringa totanus*

28CM, 11IN

Arguably the most common and widespread of British waders, breeding in damp places both near the coasts and – in smaller numbers – inland. It is a medium-sized wader, larger than a Dunlin but much smaller than a Curlew. A species that you should really get to know well, so that you can compare others with it. Two things always identify Common Redshank. One is the bright white trailing edge to the upperwing (no other common wader has this) with white rump extending up the back, and the other is the bird's distinctive call – a ringing 'tew wu wu'. There are several other waders that can be mistaken for Common Redshank – or vice versa – but there are clear differences when seen well. Non-breeding Ruff (or reeve): no wing markings and white oval on upper tail. Greenshank: greenish legs and paler, greyer plumage. Wood Sandpiper: plain wings and square white rump. This latter confusion often arises with young Common Redshank, whose legs are less bright and more yellowy, and that have spottier upperparts. (For more see those species.) Breeds widely and larger numbers winter.

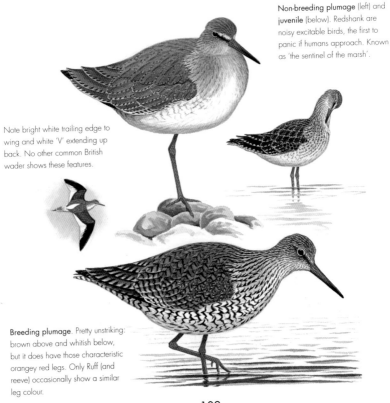

Non-breeding plumage (left) and **juvenile** (below). Redshank are noisy excitable birds, the first to panic if humans approach. Known as 'the sentinel of the marsh'.

Note bright white trailing edge to wing and white 'V' extending up back. No other common British wader shows these features.

Breeding plumage. Pretty unstriking: brown above and whitish below, but it does have those characteristic orangey red legs. Only Ruff (and reeve) occasionally show a similar leg colour.

SPOTTED REDSHANK *Tringa erythropus*

30CM, 12IN

Does not breed in Britain. A passage migrant, but not in very large numbers, mainly in southern areas, where large gatherings may occur in early autumn on estuaries, coastal marshes and occasionally inland waters. Basically similar size to Common Redshank and with red legs, but has quite a range of plumages. Breeding plumage is almost black with just a few small white spots. Non-breeding adult plumage is soft pale grey above and white below. Juveniles are brown above and most similar to Common Redshank. The easiest ways to tell them apart are as follows: Spotted Redshank has a plain upperwing (no wing bar); its bill is slightly longer and thinner; it has a narrow pale stripe above the eye and the legs are darker red. The call is quite different. Spotted Redshank give a clear 'tchuit'. The only other confusion species is Greenshank, which also lacks any wing markings. Note Greenshank's green legs, different shape and distinctive call (see page 104).

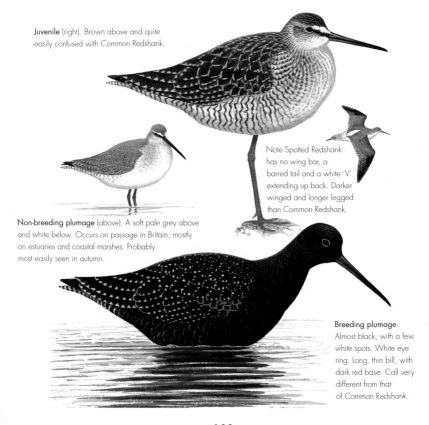

Juvenile (right). Brown above and quite easily confused with Common Redshank.

Note Spotted Redshank has no wing bar, a barred tail and a white 'V' extending up back. Darker winged and longer legged than Common Redshank.

Non-breeding plumage (above). A soft pale grey above and white below. Occurs on passage in Britain, mostly on estuaries and coastal marshes. Probably most easily seen in autumn.

Breeding plumage. Almost black, with a few white spots. White eye ring. Long, thin bill, with dark red base. Call very different from that of Common Redshank.

GREENSHANK *Tringa nebularia*

30.5CM, 12IN

A few breed in moorland and bogs of Scotland, but best known as a passage migrant in good numbers to coastal marshes and inland waters, with muddy or shingly shorelines. However, rarely do very many occur together in the same place. Slightly bigger than Common Redshank and with a squatter, less slender look. The legs are indeed a rather greyish-green and the bill is also greyer than Common Redshank's, a little thicker and slightly upturned. The plumage is greyer above and whiter below. This pale look helps pick out Greenshank even at a distance. Twisting and erratic, rapid flight. In flight, there is no white wing bar or trailing edge, but there is a white rump extending up the back. This is a similar flight pattern to that of Spotted Redshank, so note leg colour and listen for the call. Greenshank gives a clear 'tu tu tu', with a drier, less ringing quality than Common Redshank. Often chases insects across the surface of shallow water, looking rather as if it is hoovering!

Adult non-breeding plumage (above). Juvenile (far left) on back has slightly more regular pattern of dark feathers. In flight, note white rump extending up back and compare with Common and Spotted Redshanks.

Breeding plumage. A paler bird than Common Redshank, slightly bigger, with thicker, upturned bill. Outside the breeding season a bird of estuaries, saltmarshes and the edges of inland waters.

GREEN SANDPIPER *Tringa ochropus*

23CM, 9IN

Basically a dark version of the Common Sandpiper. The upperparts are really nearer black than green (in fact, they are very dark olive tinged). Has very occasionally bred in northern Britain, but is mainly a passage migrant, especially in early autumn, and a few winter in the south. Easily separated from Common Sandpiper when it flies by its black wings (above and below) and gleaming white rump. It also invariably gives a rather panicky 'tweet wheet weet' call. Green Sandpipers occur on inland waters and tidal creeks and have a tendency to hide away under banks (or seemingly always around the next bend!). If seen with Common Sandpiper it is clear that Green is a little larger and bulkier, but this isn't always obvious with a single bird. Wood Sandpiper is about the same size, but prefers shallow fresh marshes, and has less black upperparts and a quite different call (see page 106).

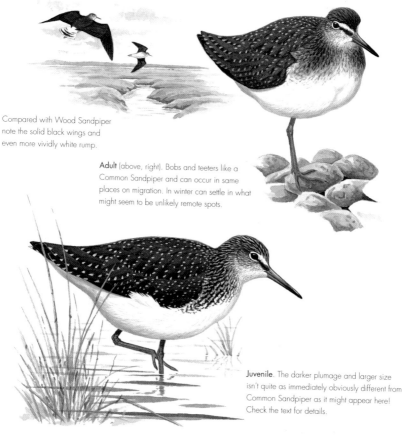

Compared with Wood Sandpiper note the solid black wings and even more vividly white rump.

Adult (above, right). Bobs and teeters like a Common Sandpiper and can occur in same places on migration. In winter can settle in what might seem to be unlikely remote spots.

Juvenile. The darker plumage and larger size isn't quite as immediately obviously different from Common Sandpiper as it might appear here! Check the text for details.

WOOD SANDPIPER *Tringa glareola*

20CM, 8IN

A few pairs breed in remote boggy areas of Scotland and the Northern Isles, but it is best known as a passage migrant, more common in autumn than spring. Prefers freshwater marshes, where it will more readily wade in shallow water than Common or Green Sandpipers. Size and plumage similar to Green Sandpiper's, but the upperparts of Wood are browner, with more distinct spotting, clearer feather edges and paler legs, which can look quite yellowish. Towering flight if flushed. In flight, it too has a square white rump, but the wings are brown above and much paler underneath than Green Sandpiper's. The call is very distinctive: a dry 'chiff if if'. Juvenile looks very like adult. Juvenile Common Redshank look not dissimilar to Wood Sandpiper – they are shorter billed and spottier on the back than adult Common Redshank, and with duller leg colour. However, note the flight pattern: Common Redshank always shows a white trailing edge to the wing and white rump extending in a 'V' up the back.

Compared with Green Sandpiper, note paler wings, especially underneath, and a completely different call, 'chiff if if'.

Juvenile (left). Very similar to adult – slightly darker. Prefers damper, marshier habitat than does either Green or Common Sandpiper and is therefore less likely to give good views.

Adult. Much more likely to be seen on autumn passage than at other times of year. Readily wades in shallow water, feeding in freshwater marshes.

COMMON SANDPIPER *Actitis hypoleucos*

20CM, 7.75IN

A small wader that is a summer visitor to Britain, breeding near streams, rivers and lakes, in moorland and hill country. It also occurs as a passage migrant at inland waters, including concrete-sided reservoirs, and at coastal marshes. However, it very rarely feeds out on mudflats, more typically sticking to creek edges or banks, even when they are dry and stony. Rather nondescript plumage: soft olive-brown above and white below, with smudged sides to the breast. However, it does have a very distinctive style, bobbing and wagging its tail as it walks, and even at rest (known as teetering). In flight, it holds its wings down, and flits over the water with a flick and glide movement. It almost invariably calls as it flies: a thin 'sweeweeweewee'. All in all, one of those birds whose jizz and habits are more distinctive than its plumage. On the ground, it is not dissimilar to both Green and Wood Sandpipers, but both those species show plain upperwings and conspicuous square white rumps in flight.

In flight, the wings are held down as it flits over the water with a flick and glide movement. No white rump. Calls as it flies.

Juvenile. In summer it occurs on upland streams: as a migrant it turns up on inland waters such as reservoirs, as well as coastal marshes, where it feeds in creeks.

Breeding plumage. Olive-brown above, white below. Note smudged breast. Distinctive jizz, constantly bobbing and wagging tail as it walks along the edges of streams and other areas of water.

107

TURNSTONE *Arenaria interpres*

23CM, 9IN

A very distinctive, dumpy, short-legged little wader, with a 'tortoiseshell' plumage. Does not breed in Britain, but is well distributed around the coasts, even in summer. Has a very definite preference for rocky or pebbly shores, where it feeds by rummaging among seaweed. Also feeds on the strand-line, turning debris to look for invertebrates. Very occasionally occurs on inland waters, but again will stick to pebbles or concrete. Note the distinctive short, wedge-shaped bill and short orange legs. Non-breeding plumage birds are dark greyish-brown above with white on the face and underparts. They often share the same rocky places as Purple Sandpipers and look a bit like them, but note the orange (not yellow) legs and distinctive shape. Purple Sandpipers are also much rarer winter visitors (see page 92). Breeding-plumage Turnstone have lovely 'broken' patterns of black, white and orange. You often also see sort of 'in-between' plumages. Turnstone's call is almost impossible to write down, but is a distinctive chattering, 'kit it it it'.

Juvenile (below). Prefers rocky shores and pebbly beaches. Feeds on insects and other invertebrates, which it finds by turning over pebbles, seaweed and debris on the tide-line.

Winter plumage (above) Occurs in all sorts of mottled plumage, though winter plumage is greyish-brown. May be seen in company with Purple Sandpiper, which likes the same rocky habitat.

Breeding plumage (right). Comprises rich tortoiseshell pattern of chestnut, black and white. Orange legs and short bill. Does not breed in Britain, but still seen in summer on coasts.

GREAT SKUA *Stercorarius skua*

58CM, 23IN

Skuas are gull-like seabirds, but with a faster, more agile flight style, suited to their habit of harassing other birds into dropping or regurgitating their food. This is known as klepto-parasitism (translated as feeding by stealing). As the name implies, Great Skua is the largest of the skuas. It is quite a bit bigger and bulkier than Arctic Skua (see page 110), but the difference isn't always immediately obvious with single birds. Great Skuas breed on coastal bog and moorland in the Northern Isles. They are known locally as Bonxies. Like all skuas, they will dive bomb you if you walk through a colony – quite a frightening experience. Also occurs on seawatches in spring and autumn. Dark chocolatey brown, often with paler blotching on the head and face. Large immature gulls (Herring and Lesser Black-backed) can look almost as brown and are about the same size, and therefore can be mistaken for Great Skuas. Note the Great Skua's short, wedge-shaped tail. Young gulls also have paler upper tails and less completely dark plumage.

The bright white wing patches are conspicuous even at long range and very useful on a seawatch. Flight is heavier, steadier and less erratic than that of other skuas.

Only one colour phase, but plumage varies. Some individuals are dark chocolate-brown, others have almost golden tinges. Great Skuas dive at intruders on their breeding grounds.

ARCTIC SKUA *Sterocarius parasiticus*

46CM, 18IN

You are most likely to see skuas either in the Northern Isles, where they breed, or on a seawatch, most commonly off a headland, with an onshore wind, in spring or autumn. Four species occur in Britain, but Arctic is by far the most common. It's not a bad rule to assume that if you see a skua, it's an Arctic until proved otherwise. Arctic Skua is smaller than a Herring Gull and clearly smaller than Great Skua (see page 109). Birds occur in various plumages, from dark phase (can look almost black) to light phase (brown above, whitish below), and even intermediates. Juveniles are brown and barred. Pomarine and Long-tailed Skuas have similar colour phases so it's hard to separate them on plumage. Juvenile gulls and Gannets can look very dark, especially against the sun, and can be mistaken for skuas. Gulls even sometimes behave like skuas, chasing other birds (see pages 120–1). When it comes to seawatching, the trick is to get as much experience as possible; always consider the possible confusion species.

Note the elongated but fairly short central tail feathers of Arctic (right), compared with the streamers of Long-tailed, and the 'spoons' of Pomarine.

Juvenile plumage. Brown and barred. Arctic Skuas breed on the islands around Scotland and occur elsewhere in Britain as passage migrants.

Plumage is very variable, from dark phase to **light phase** shown here. Can be confused with immature gulls and Gannets as well other skuas. More buoyant, graceful flight than Great Skua's.

110

POMARINE SKUA *Stercorarius pomarinus*

54CM, 21IN

Does not breed in Britain, but occurs on migration. Often travels in quite large flocks, which are seen offshore, especially in May, off the south and east coasts, and the Outer Hebrides. Each year, new seawatching sites are tried, and new skua routes discovered. Autumn passage is less predictable, and this species can occur from August right through to November. At all times, remember that Pomarine is a rarer bird than Arctic Skua. It occurs in dark and light phases, and the juveniles are barred. Adults have central tail feathers with 'spoons', which are noticeable at long range, even if the impression is simply of a peculiarly elongated tail. Without the spoons, however, Pomarine is difficult to separate from Arctic Skua. Pomarine is slightly larger, rather more barrel chested and has a slightly steadier wingbeat (often likened to a large gull's), but it takes experience to sort them out and sometimes even experts disagree.

Experienced seawatchers can usually make out the heavier, more barrel-chested build of Pomarine Skua compared with Arctic, but even so, wind strength and distance make it difficult.

Juvenile plumage. Brown and barred, and difficult to separate from Arctic Skua.

Like Arctic Skua, Pomarine occurs in both a dark and a **light phase** (right). This is not a British breeding bird, but a passage migrant seen off the coasts.

COMMON GULL *Larus canus*

41CM, 16IN

The second most numerous of the small gulls. Breeds in the north of Britain, often in delightfully wild countryside, but takes to playing fields and farmland in winter. Often in company of Black-headed Gulls. Common Gull is larger than Black-headed, but considerably smaller than the 'big gulls' (Herring and Lesser Black-backed). The plumage and shape, however, are rather more similar to a small Herring Gull's. Amongst Black-headeds, adult Commons are distinguished by their larger size, lack of head markings, slightly darker grey back, and yellowy bill and legs. The wings have black tips to the primaries, with white spots or 'mirrors'. No white wedge on the underwing. Young Common Gulls start brownish, then acquire a grey back, before eventually moulting into adult plumage. The call is a fairly gentle mewing. The most similar species is probably Kittiwake, but Kittiwakes are exclusively birds of rocky coasts, and have black legs and solid black wing tips.

In flight, wings show black tips with white spots or 'mirrors'. **Young birds** (far right) gradually become greyer through the **second winter** (near right) to the **winter adult** (bottom, right), which just has a streaked head.

Young Common Gull (left). Brownish, then acquires grey back, before eventually moulting into adult plumage. Bill and legs are pinkish or greyish-pink, and bill often has a blackish tip.

Adult. Larger than Black-headed; looks rather like a small Herring Gull, but has a more gentle expression. Common has a yellow bill and legs.

KITTIWAKE *Rissa tridactyla*

41CM, 16IN

A small gull that looks rather similar to a Common Gull, but has very different habits and habitat preference. Kittiwakes breed on sea cliffs – often in very large colonies – and winter largely out to sea. Very rarely recorded inland, usually only when storm driven. Even at the coast, they seem loath to get away from rocks or jetties; some even nest on quayside buildings. A common sight on a seawatch, so need to be distinguished from Common Gull. Note wing pattern. Adult Kittiwake has a solid, dipped-in-ink black wing tip: a feature surprisingly easy to appreciate even at long range. Juvenile Kittiwakes have a very distinctive black 'W' pattern on their upperwings, a black half collar on the hind neck and a black tail band. This plumage is similar to Little Gull's, but Kittiwake is clearly larger and with a less fluttery flight. Kittiwakes very obligingly remind us of their name by calling 'kitti wake kitti wake'.

Compared with Common Gull, note solid inky black wing tip. **Juvenile** (below, right) has black 'W' pattern on upperwings, black half collar and black tail band.

Breeds in large colonies on sea cliffs. At closer range or at rest, note that the bill is yellow but the feet are black (greeny yellow in Common Gull).

BLACK-HEADED GULL *Chroicocephalus ridibundus*

35–38CM, 14–15IN

Black-headed Gull is by far the most common of Britain's small gulls. It is found all the year round, all over Britain, breeding both at coastal marshes and by inland waters. In winter, it often feeds on playing fields, farmland and rubbish dumps. Black-headed Gull only has the black (actually chocolate-brown) head in breeding plumage. In non-breeding plumage, there is a blackish spot behind the eye. Very young birds are blotchy gingery brown on the upperparts. As they get older, the darker markings are reduced to bars on the upperwing and at the end of the tail (this is often referred to as first-winter plumage). If this sounds complicated, don't panic! Several key identification points don't change (see captions). The calls are a raucous screeching: the birds always sound bad tempered.

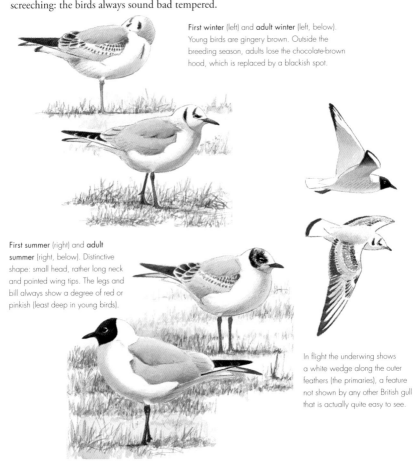

First winter (left) and adult winter (left, below). Young birds are gingery brown. Outside the breeding season, adults lose the chocolate-brown hood, which is replaced by a blackish spot.

First summer (right) and adult summer (right, below). Distinctive shape: small head, rather long neck and pointed wing tips. The legs and bill always show a degree of red or pinkish (least deep in young birds).

In flight the underwing shows a white wedge along the outer feathers (the primaries), a feature not shown by any other British gull that is actually quite easy to see.

MEDITERRANEAN GULL *Larus melanocephalus*

39CM, 15IN

The first step in gull identification is to separate the various species into small and large gulls. The second step is to get to know the most common species, and compare others with them. A major key to gull identification is to realize that all gulls have several plumages that can look very different at various stages: breeding and non-breeding, and various stages of juvenile plumage, for gulls may take several years to reach maturity. The Mediterranean Gull, though rare, is always worth keeping your eyes peeled for at a gull roost. Although it breeds in extremely small numbers, it is slightly more common in winter and young birds may be seen in late spring. Compare with both Black-headed (with which this species occasionally breeds) and Common Gulls. Note adult has no black on wings, and white forewing rather than the pale leading edge of Black-headed. Red bill and long red legs. In winter plumage, very pale with 'pirate's patch' smudging eye. In flight has shallower wingbeats than Common Gull.

Adult in summer (above, left) has a black hood, more extensive than Black-headed Gull's. Note pale forewing – no black tips to primaries. **Second-year birds** (above, centre and far right), however, do show black wing tips. They are most likely to be confused with juvenile Common Gulls.

Compare **juvenile** (foreground) with **adult** at rear. Note patch over eye.

HERRING GULL *Larus argentatus*

56–66CM, 22–26IN

The most widespread of the big gulls. Nests all around the coast, often in large colonies, and winters everywhere, including inland on fields and rubbish dumps. Large roosts occur on reservoirs and lakes. Although the plumage is not dissimilar to Common Gull's, Herring is much bigger. Adults have a grey back, white underparts and black wing tips with white spots, or 'mirrors'. Note leg colour is pinkish. Most similar species is Lesser Black-backed Gull (see page 118), which has a darker back (but not actually black) and yellow legs. Juvenile large gulls are less easy to identify. Any flock of large gulls is likely to have birds in various plumages, so it's important to appreciate the typical size and jizz of any one species. Herring Gull is a little larger than Lesser Black-backed, but clearly smaller than Great Black-backed. Juvenile plumages tend to be less dark than plumages of either of the Black-backeds. Call: the familiar seagull cry.

Juvenile (near right). In flight has a darker forewing than adult (far right), and a dark tail band. Note white spots ('mirrors') on adult's wing tips. Strong flyer, with much soaring and gliding.

Adult (top). Larger than Lesser Black-backed; grey back, yellow bill and eye, and pinkish legs. Black wing tips with white spots.

Juvenile. Herring Gulls take four years to reach maturity, and become gradually greyer throughout this period until they attain full adult plumage.

Really young Herring Gulls are blotchy brown, with blackish wing markings and tail band. Then, at the **intermediate plumage** stage (above), the greyer feathers begin to appear, firstly on the back.

116

LITTLE GULL *Hydrocoloeus minutus*

28CM, 11IN

As the name implies, the smallest British gull. It looks rather like a tiny Black-headed Gull, but is much rarer. Little Gulls do not breed in Britain, but there is a large population in Holland, which passes along our east coast in spring and autumn, sometimes in quite large numbers. East winds may drift flocks well inland to reservoirs or lakes. There are also wintering flocks in one or two favoured locations in the Irish Sea. Nevertheless, it is quite possible to pass a year's birding in Britain without seeing a Little Gull. Breeding-plumage adults have a completely black hood, white wing tips and a rather unexpected dusky grey underwing. In non-breeding plumage the hood is reduced to a black cap and a black spot behind the eye. Juveniles – the likeliest plumage in autumn – have blackish backs and caps and a dark 'W' marking across the wings. This plumage is very similar to juvenile Kittiwake's (see page 113), but Kittiwakes are very rare away from the sea.

In flight, **juvenile** (near right) shows dark 'W' across the wings, as in Kittiwake. Look for the darker back (mantle) of Little Gull and the fluttery flight. **Breeding-plumage adult** (far right) shows dark underwing.

Juvenile (below) has a blackish cap and spot behind the eye. In **intermediate plumages** (left) fewer black markings than in juveniles.

Breeding-plumage adult (left). Looks like a tiny Black-headed Gull. Little Gulls do not breed in Britain, although they do in Holland. They winter at sea.

117

LESSER BLACK-BACKED GULL *Larus fuscus*

53–56CM, 21–22IN

Most numerous during the summer, when it breeds on northern coasts and even inland moorlands, most commonly in the north of Britain, although it is spreading. Increasingly present during the winter months, in similar habitats to Herring Gull. Adults distinguished from Herring Gull by darker back (mantle). Some of them (Scandinavian race) are almost black, but others are merely dark grey, but always darker than Herring Gull. Lesser Black-backed also has yellow legs (pink in Herring). Juveniles have the same range of plumages as Herring Gull, taking four years to become fully adult, but Lesser Black-backed is generally rather darker, especially on the wings. Lesser Black-backed is a little smaller and slimmer than Herring Gull, but this isn't always easy to appreciate unless the species are together. To separate from Great Black-backed: Lesser is considerably smaller, Great has a blacker back, but with more white patches, and pink legs. Juveniles have whiter heads (see Great Black-backed). Call: similar to Herring Gull's.

Occurs throughout the year, in similar habitats to Herring Gull, but may breed near inland waters.

Adult (below). Yellow bill, eyes and legs. Depth of colour on back variable from almost black to dark grey, depending on race.

Like Herring Gull, Lesser Black-backed takes four years to reach maturity, and its plumage gradually changes from brown to **adult's** dark grey and white (top).

Juvenile (left and above). Tends to be darker than young Herring Gulls, especially on the wings, but this is variable and sometimes immature birds of the two species are indistinguishable in the field.

118

GREAT BLACK-BACKED GULL *Larus marinus*

64–79CM, 25–31IN

As the name implies, larger – considerably so – than Lesser Black-backed. Adults have really black backs, but have more white flecks on the closed wing. Bill and eyes are yellow, but the legs are pink (yellow in Lesser). Juveniles have whiter heads than Lesser or Herring, and bolder black-and-white chequered upperparts. Great Black-backeds breed on rocky coasts, cliffs and islands, but rarely in such large colonies as the other big gulls. They winter on estuaries and marshes, but are much scarcer inland. A black-backed gull inland is most likely to be a Lesser. The call has a deep, almost goose-like quality.

Much more exclusively coastal than the other large gulls. **Adult** (below and far right) is darker than Lesser Black-backed.

Compare whiter head and underparts of **immature birds** (left and below) with both Lesser Black-backed and Herring Gulls.

Great Black-backeds feed on a wide variety of animals; they can be seen hawking for flying ants or prowling Puffin colonies for both young and unwary adult birds.

Final warning note on big gulls. In flight, especially going to roost or on migration, flocks often fly in 'V' formation. At a distance, they can easily be mistaken for geese. A proper scrutiny soon reveals their longer, slimmer wings and obvious beaks.

SIMILAR SPECIES: SEABIRDS IN FLIGHT

On a seawatch, birds are often seen at a distance or against the light, thus making identification tricky. If you think you may have spotted one of the scarcer seabirds – a skua or shearwater – check that it isn't a more common species.

Juvenile Lesser Black-backed Gulls are typical impersonators of Arctic Skuas, particularly when silhouetted against the sun. Gannet in dark juvenile plumage is another Skua impersonator.

Juvenile Lesser Black-backed Gull

Adult Great Black-backed Gull

Juvenile Gannet

Adult Arctic Skua

Fulmar

Guillemot

Sooty Shearwater

Manx Shearwater

Many seabirds look basically dark above and white below. Both shearwaters and Fulmars fly with a stiff-winged gliding style, while auks (guillemots, etc) fly on fast-whirring wings.

Seabird plumages vary considerably with age (and indeed with the effects of the light and at long distance), and skuas even occur in various different phases, so jizz is all important.

Adult Great Black-backed Gull

Adult Lesser Black-backed Gull

Adult dark phase Pomarine Skua

Juvenile Arctic Skua

Juvenile Lesser Black-backed Gull

Juvenile Gannet

2nd year Gannet

Great Skua

Juvenile Herring Gull

Pale immature Pomarine Skua

Note the flight styles: are the wings stiff (like a glider's – or shearwater's) or flappy (like a gull's or skua's)? Some birds – like Gannets – employ a bit of both.

COMMON TERN *Sterna hirundo*

35CM, 14IN

Terns are smaller and more slender than gulls, with slimmer wings and a faster flight style that often involves hovering or skimming over the water when feeding. They are all summer visitors to Britain, arriving in April or May and very rarely seen after late September to early October. Size, bill and leg colour are important when separating the species. Common Terns breed around the coast, frequently in colonies, and also increasingly on inland waters, often on specially provided rafts. It's not a bad rule to assume that a 'white' tern inland is most likely to be a Common. Like other tern species, it has a black cap. In late autumn the forehead becomes whiter; the bill and legs darker. (See also Roseate Tern, opposite.) Common *is* most common, except in the north of Britain, where Arctic Tern takes over. Inland, Arctics occur on passage, but are nothing like as frequent as Common. Roseate is rare, usually seen in a few favoured locations only. Common Tern's call is a harsh 'skeee ar' or a short 'ki kik'.

The best feature in flight is a dark wedge on the upperwing, on the outer primary feathers, which Arctic lacks.

Adult non-breeding plumage (right) in late autumn. The forehead goes whiter and the bill and legs darker.

Juvenile. White forehead and dark wing markings. Juvenile and non-breeding Common and Arctic Terns are hard to separate.

Breeding plumage. The bill is scarlet with a black tip, and the legs are also scarlet. The very similar Arctic Tern has a deeper blood-red bill and legs.

ARCTIC TERN *Sterna paradisaea*

35CM, 14IN

Arctic Tern breeds on the coast (and occasionally inland) in the north of Britain, where Common becomes scarcer. Arctics are usually in larger colonies. They occur on inland waters on passage, particularly in spring. Looks very similar to Common Tern. The calls are very similar to Common Tern's: 'kee ar' and 'kik kik'. The champion migrant, some birds breed in the Arctic and winter in the Antarctic.

Juvenile

Adult lacks a dark primary wedge on the upperwing. **Juveniles** similar to Common Tern, but the trailing edge to the upperwing is cleaner white.

Breeding plumage. Very similar to Common Tern, but in breeding plumage the bill is dark blood red and has no black tip. Slightly shorter legs, also dark red; generally has longer tail streamers.

ROSEATE TERN *Sterna dougallii*

38CM, 15IN

The rarest of the medium-sized 'white' terns. Breeds in a very few well-known and well-protected sites. In breeding plumage looks similar to Common (and Arctic) Terns, but is brighter white, especially on the upper wings, and is slightly larger and more slender, with longer tail streamers. The call is a distinctive rasping sound, sometimes likened to a tarpaulin being torn.

Juvenile (left). Looks more black and white than other young terns, with stronger black chequering on the back, black legs and a fuller black cap.

Breeding plumage (left). Bill is almost black, with just a flush of red at the base. Legs are red. The breast sometimes shows a pinkish (roseate) flush.

123

SANDWICH TERN *Sterna sandvicensis*

42CM, 16.5IN

The largest of the 'white', black-capped terns. Clearly bigger than Common, Arctic and Roseate, with long, thin wings, a less deeply forked tail and a shaggy crest. Adults have a black bill with a yellow tip and black legs. Non-breeding and juvenile birds have a white forehead, and very young birds have black chequering on the back. The call is a harsh 'kirrick' (clearly different from the calls of other terns). The youngsters also give a thin squeaking, which is especially heard in autumn. Sandwich Terns arrive earlier than the other species and stay later, very occasionally even wintering. They are very much coastal birds, though they prefer sandy or grassy – rather than rocky – breeding areas. They are very unusual on inland waters, though sometimes come through on passage. Flying past on a seawatch, their whiteness may recall Roseate Tern, but Sandwich is clearly larger and slimmer – and much more common. When diving to feed, plunges from a greater height than other terns.

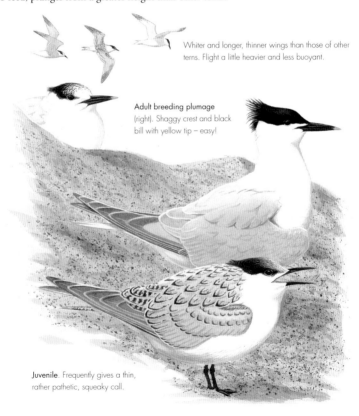

Whiter and longer, thinner wings than those of other terns. Flight a little heavier and less buoyant.

Adult breeding plumage (right). Shaggy crest and black bill with yellow tip – easy!

Juvenile. Frequently gives a thin, rather pathetic, squeaky call.

LITTLE TERN *Sternula albifrons*

24CM, 9.5IN

By far the smallest of the black-capped 'white' terns, with a very fast, flapping flight style, involving much hovering and plunge diving when feeding. It tends to feed in shallower water than other tern species, often at the breakwater. The forehead is white in all plumages. In breeding plumage, the bill is bright yellow with a black tip, and the legs are yellow. Bill and legs are duller in juveniles than adults, and juveniles also have brown markings on the back and upperwings. The call is a high-pitched 'kik ki kik'. All in all, not a difficult bird to identify. Little Terns breed around the coasts of Britain, nesting in shallow scrapes, but their preference for sandy or shingly beaches makes them very vulnerable to human disturbance, and their numbers are decreasing where they are not fully protected. They are very scarce on inland waters. Like Sandwich Terns they fly out to West Africa for the winter. Young birds take two years to reach maturity and return to their place of birth.

Flying with fast, flickering wingbeats, Little Terns feed with much hovering and plunge diving, often into waves breaking close to the shore.

Winter-type plumage (left). This is very rarely seen in Britain. **Juvenile** (below). Don't worry too much about plumage details. Its small size makes it pretty unmistakable.

Adult breeding plumage (right). Neat white forehead, yellow bill and tiny size – nothing else like it.

BLACK TERN *Chlidonias niger*

24CM, 9.5IN

Belongs to the group known as 'marsh terns'. Black Terns breed as nearby as Holland, but have not nested regularly in Britain since the 19th century. They are fairly common on passage, particularly in late April and May, over inland lakes and marshes by the coast, and sometimes offshore with other seabirds. Juveniles and non-breeding adults can be puzzling. Compared with Common and Arctic Terns, Black Tern is smaller, with darker grey upperparts, dark rump, short, almost square-ended tail and small black half collar on the shoulder. This plumage is a little reminiscent of some Little Gull plumages (see page 117) but juvenile Little Gulls have a striking black 'W' on the upperwing, while non-breeding adults have paler upperwings than those of Black Terns. Adult Black Terns coming out of breeding plumage (usually seen in July or early August) can look very blotchy, with patches of black and white on their bodies. When feeding they skim and dip to take food off the water's surface. Call: a soft 'kik kik'.

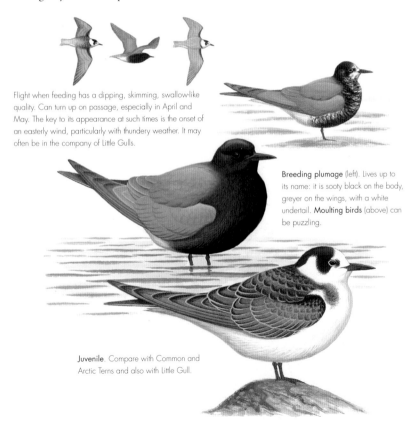

Flight when feeding has a dipping, skimming, swallow-like quality. Can turn up on passage, especially in April and May. The key to its appearance at such times is the onset of an easterly wind, particularly with thundery weather. It may often be in the company of Little Gulls.

Breeding plumage (left). Lives up to its name: it is sooty black on the body, greyer on the wings, with a white undertail. **Moulting birds** (above) can be puzzling.

Juvenile. Compare with Common and Arctic Terns and also with Little Gull.

126

SUMMER ADULTS

Little Tern

Sandwich Tern

Common Tern

Little Gull

Arctic Tern

Kittiwake

Roseate Tern

Terns are more buoyant and slender-winged than even Kittiwakes and Little Gulls. Flight identification of terns is tricky, especially in juvenile plumage. Note the wing markings of the various species.

JUVENILE PLUMAGE
Black Tern

Arctic Tern

Sandwich Tern

Little Tern

Roseate Tern

1st winter
Little Gull

Common Tern

Kittiwake

ADULTS WINTER/
LATE AUTUMN

Little Gull

Common Tern

Sandwich Tern

Arctic Tern

COMMON GUILLEMOT *Uria aalge*

42CM, 16.5IN

Belongs to the family known as auks (the northern hemisphere equivalent of penguins, except that they can fly). Widespread, breeding around the coasts on steep rocky cliff ledges, sometimes in very large colonies. The other common British auks are Razorbill and Puffin. All are easy to identify at close quarters. Note Common Guillemot's browner plumage and thin, pointed beak. Some individuals have white 'spectacles' and are known as 'bridled'. However, when seen flying by on a seawatch, or at a distance on the sea, auks are not so easy to identify. With practice, you can notice the guillemot's more cigar-shaped body and browner plumage. In winter plumage the face becomes whiter. Distant birds on the water can be mistaken for small seaducks or even grebes (see page 47). Auks spend much of their winter way out on the ocean; at this time they are much less numerous around British coasts than in the breeding season or on passage.

In flight, pointed at both ends. Distant flying auks are hard to identify. Young flutter off the ledges for their first winter at sea before they can fly properly.

Breeding plumage (left). Some birds have white 'spectacles' and are known as 'bridled' guillemots. Breeds on cliff ledges, laying a single egg, pointed so that it rolls on its own axis.

Non-breeding plumage (below). The face becomes white in winter. Guillemots spend much of the autumn and winter far out to sea. They feed on fish, diving from the water's surface.

RAZORBILL *Alca torda*

41CM, 16IN

Similar habits and plumage to Common Guillemot, but generally not quite as numerous around our coasts, though we do have a large percentage of the world's population breeding in Britain, on rocky cliffs. Razorbills favour less exposed places than the guillemots, preferring to nest in crevices rather than on ledges. The plumage is blacker than Common Guillemot's, and the bill is a deep (old-fashioned razor) shape, with white bands on it and a white eyestreak above. The bill is, however, not as parrot-like as a Puffin's, and a Puffin also has a white face. Razorbills tend to swim with their tails cocked and they look a little stockier than Common Guillemots. At distance or in flight, they usually look blacker than Common Guillemots, and with less pointed ends. The face becomes white in winter and – like other auks – from a distance they can be mistaken for seaducks on the water (see page 47). Young birds have smaller bills than adults, and like young guillemots, they launch themselves off a cliff-face before they can fly properly, to winter at sea with their parents.

Blacker than Common Guillemot and a little less cigar-shaped, but they are not easy to separate in flight.

Breeding plumage (left). Stubbier beak than Common Guillemot's, but still nothing like a Puffin's. Nests in crevices on cliffs in loose colonies, often higher up than Common Guillemots.

Non-breeding plumage (below). Face becomes white in winter. Dives from water's surface; underwater swims with its wings, like a penguin.

BLACK GUILLEMOT *Cepphus grylle*

34CM, 13.5IN

Often called Tystie (its old Norse name). Breeds on rocky coasts, mainly in the north of Britain and in Ireland. Nests in crevices and caves, and is not as obviously colonial as the other auks. Similar shape to a Common Guillemot (pointed beak), but considerably smaller. Breeding plumage is very distinctive – velvety black, with red feet and inside to the mouth, and with a bright white wing patch. Winter and juvenile plumages are quite different: messily whitish, with variable dark grey on head, back and flanks. This resembles some plumages of Long-tailed Duck, especially if the bird is diving on the sea at a distance. The breeding plumage is not dissimilar to male Velvet Scoter's (see page 31), but these birds are much bigger and have white head markings, and in fact the white wing patch is on the speculum. Black Guillemot is rarely involved in seabird movements like the other auks, and is scarce in southern waters.

Flights are usually short. Rarely seen on seawatches with other auks. Tends to stay closer to shore.

Breeding plumage. Very pretty – it's a shame it tends to hide in crevices. Note the pointed bill. Does not breed in large colonies, but in groups of a few pairs.

Non-breeding plumage. At its whitest in mid-winter. Very variable according to stage of moult, but white wing flash is retained.

PUFFIN *Fratercula arctica*

30CM, 12IN

One of Britain's best-loved and most recognizable birds. Breeds on the coast and on islands around Britain, most commonly in the north. It actually nests in deep crevices or underground, often in rabbit burrows. Smaller than either Common Guillemot or Razorbill, with a white face and brightly coloured, parrot-like beak. Juvenile Puffins have smaller, darker bills and greyer cheeks than adults, and are therefore nothing like as distinctive as their parents. Puffins are by no means as easily or as frequently seen as Common Guillemots and Razorbills.

Flying by out to sea, or on the water, the small size and white face are still noticeable. Most confusable with Little Auk. Rarely seen in large numbers on seawatch.

Look for Puffins on clifftops, where they nest under boulders or in rabbit burrows. **Adult** (above, right) is unmistakable. **Juvenile** (above) has a smaller bill and greyer cheeks than an adult.

LITTLE AUK *Alle alle*

20CM, 8IN

Very small indeed – Starling sized. Dumpy, black above, white below, with very fast-whirring wings. Little Auks occasionally occur in large numbers, mainly off the east coast, in November and sometimes other winter months. At such times flocks may be seen racing past offshore, or even tagging along with Starlings. Birds are sometimes 'wrecked' inland, and have been known to drop onto small ponds or even down into city streets. These movements are clearly triggered by certain weather patterns or food shortages, but we don't know exactly why or when they will occur.

At a distance flocks look rather like small black-and-white waders. Single bird resembles a small, fast Puffin with no visible bill.

It is possible to go for years without seeing a Little Auk, then – if you get lucky on a seawatch – you may see hundreds.

FERAL PIGEON *Columba livia* var. *domestica*

33CM, 13IN

Also referred to as London pigeon, but unfortunately – from the birdwatcher's point of view – not restricted to London. Feral pigeons occur in all sorts of plumages that can fleetingly resemble various other wild species. To make them even more confusing, flight style can resemble various unrelated species, from raptors (a single bird racing away) to waders (a low- or high-flying flock), see page 73. If you glimpse a bird you can't pin a name to, ask yourself if it could have been a feral pigeon.

The feral pigeon occurs in a variety of colours, including one that is identical to its wild ancestor, the Rock Dove (see page 230). In flight, it can be mistaken for other species.

STOCK DOVE *Columba oenas*

33CM, 13IN

Breeds in most parts of Britain, except in the far north. Nests in holes in trees in parks or on farmland. Never as numerous as Woodpigeon, though it may feed with it in mixed flocks. Smaller than Woodpigeon, lacks white on the neck and in the wing, and has a dark eye. The call is a rather owl-like, soft 'oo woo' that is quite different from the more expected cooing of a pigeon.

Similar to Rock Dove (or Rock Dove-type feral pigeons), but has only short, thin black wing bars, and a dark rump. In flight has a black trailing edge to the wings and tail.

WOODPIGEON *Columba palumbus*

41CM, 16IN

The largest of British pigeons. Common in all sorts of habitats all over the country, though understandably scarcer on some remote and generally treeless islands. Often gathers in large flocks in winter, especially on farmland, and large movements occur in the autumn, probably involving continental birds. Distinguished from Stock Dove and feral (Rock Dove-type) pigeon by large size, bright white mark on the neck, and white wing flashes when it flies (often noticeable even at rest). Juveniles lack the white neck patches, but still have the white on the wings. 'Claps' its wings noisily when disturbed as it panics away. It also claps during its display flight, which involves soaring up high then gliding down with wings held in a 'V' shape. The call is an insistent and rhythmic 'coo coo-cooo', which is relaxing or annoying, depending on your taste. Nests in trees, where it builds an untidy and flimsy platform of twigs. Feeds mostly on vegetable matter, including cereal crops, seeds and berries.

Juvenile. Woodpigeons usually lay two eggs, and like other members of the pigeon family rear their young on a substance called pigeon's milk, which is made in the adults' crops.

White crescents on wings obvious. Woodpigeons make a loud clapping noise when flushed and will also clap in display flight.

Adult. Close views – and birds in town parks are a lot tamer than their country cousins – reveal the pinkish breast and glossy metallic sheen to the sides of the neck.

133

COLLARED DOVE *Streptopelia decaocto*

32CM, 12.5IN

Although the first Collared Doves only arrived in Britain in the mid-1950s, the species has spread to most parts of the country, to the extent that these birds are now almost as familiar as Woodpigeons in some areas. Particularly fond of farmyards, the Collared Dove also breeds in gardens and parkland. Its rapid expansion in range has partly been attributed to its very long breeding season – from February to October in Britain. Slimmer and longer tailed than any of the pigeons, the Collared Dove is basically similar to the Turtle Dove, but Collared is seen all the year round (Turtle Dove is a summer visitor) and its plumage looks much smoother. Fawn above and pale grey below, with a thin black collar. More like Turtle Dove in flight, but note Collared's plainer back and wings, with only the wing tips dark, and paler tail. Both Collared and Turtle Doves have white edges to the tail when seen from above. The call is a monotonous 'koo kookok', and a rather whingey nasal 'kwerr'.

In flight similar to Turtle Dove, but note plainer back and wings. Has broader but less bright white tail band than Turtle Dove.

Collared Doves often choose dense conifer trees to nest in. They usually have two broods per year, but as many as five have been attempted.

Juvenile (left) is greyer on the back than adult (below, left), with a less well-developed half collar.

TURTLE DOVE *Streptopelia turtur*

27CM, 11IN

The other small dove in Britain. A summer visitor only, and in sadly decreasing numbers. Arrives late April or May. More often heard than seen – the call is a lovely gentle purring. If seen in flight, it has a very fast style, with an even quicker flap than Collared Dove. The scaly feathering on the back and wings, darker trailing edge to the wing, bright white undertail and black tail centre all give it a less bland look than that of Collared Dove. Seen at rest, the plumage has a lovely pale chestnut warmth to it, and there is a black-and-white neck patch. Like Collared Dove, it shows a white outer tail when seen from above, but the centre of the tail is black. Most common in southern and eastern Britain, and quite scarce in Scotland and Ireland. Although it nests deep in trees and hedges, migrants may occur at the coast in more open habitat such as stubble fields.

Fast in flight. Spangled back; white edges and dark centre to tail give the bird a diamond shape when it is taking off from the ground. More contrasting white undertail than in Collared Dove.

Juvenile similar to **adult** (pair above), but slightly paler and greyer and without neck bars. Found mostly in the south and east of England; feeds mainly on weed seeds.

CUCKOO *Cuculus canorus*

33CM, 13IN

Everyone knows the Cuckoo's call and is aware of its habit of laying eggs in other birds' nests, but this is a surprisingly hard species to actually see. Cuckoos are purely summer visitors, arriving in mid-April and usually gone before the end of September. You are most likely to see one in flight, especially as it crosses open habitat such as a reedbed (one of the Cuckoo's favourite host species is Reed Warbler). Notice the long tapering tail and the droopy-winged look. The barred underparts are similar to a Sparrowhawk's (see page 65). Adults are grey, but juveniles are rich brown, with a white spot on the back of the neck. There is also a very rare bright rufous female adult form. As well as the familiar 'cuckoo', females also have a strange bubbling call, sometimes heard in spring. Cuckoos feed on insects and particularly hairy caterpillars, so they do spend time on the ground. Females lay eggs in several nests over the course of a number of days, and are often mobbed by small birds.

The flight is fast and shallow-winged and this – coupled with the slim build and long tail – gives it a rather hawk-like jizz.

Female (left). Rare rufous form. Grey-form female is slightly browner than male (see below).

Adult male (above). Grey as is grey-form female, which also has a brownish wash on the breast and browner looking flight feathers.
Juvenile (left). Rich brown with a white patch on the nape.

BARN OWL *Tyto alba*

34CM, 13.5IN

Although like all owls, Barn Owls are largely nocturnal, they also hunt at dawn and dusk, sometimes until the sun is well up. In flight, they look a ghostly white, although in fact the back is a gentle honey colour. The face is more oval-shaped than the faces of other owls. Barn Owls hunt over fields and along roadsides, so your best chance of seeing them is often from a car. It also means that – sadly – many of them end up as road kills. The only other white-looking owl is the very rare Snowy Owl (see page 231), which is much bigger and seen only occasionally in Scotland and the Northern Isles. Barn Owls do not hoot: they produce various eerie shrieks, as well as hissing and snoring noises.

They breed in hollow trees, old barns and – increasingly – specially provided nesting boxes. Found in most parts of Britain and Ireland, but scarce in northern Scotland.

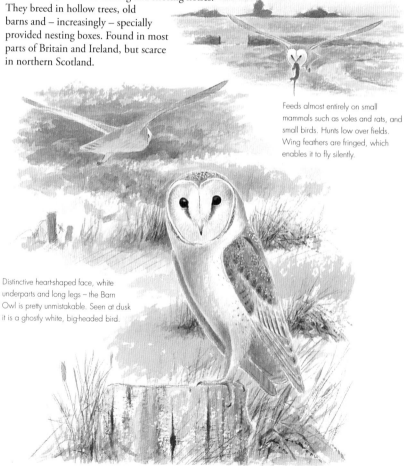

Feeds almost entirely on small mammals such as voles and rats, and small birds. Hunts low over fields. Wing feathers are fringed, which enables it to fly silently.

Distinctive heart-shaped face, white underparts and long legs – the Barn Owl is pretty unmistakable. Seen at dusk it is a ghostly white, big-headed bird.

137

LITTLE OWL *Athene noctua*

22CM, 8.5IN

Widespread in Britain (except Ireland) but perhaps becoming scarcer. Not a true native, it was introduced from the 1840s onwards with the object of reducing garden pests; it feeds on insects, small mammals and birds. Little Owls often roost during the day in surprisingly conspicuous places, such as on barn roofs, walls, cliffs and bare trees, and they sometimes draw attention to themselves by calling. They give a rather mewing, repeated 'kee u kee u'. They really are little – barely half the size of a Tawny Owl – and the most obvious feature is the face pattern of whitish eyebrows and chinstrap, and piercing yellow eyes. They often bob when alarmed. The flight is a fast flap and glide, often close to the ground, before they swoop back up onto a perch. Probably the best place to look for them is established hedgerows with gnarled or even dead tree trunks in them. They are also fond of quarries. They nest mainly in tree holes, but also take to specially provided nest boxes.

Fast, flapping flight, and glide, close to ground, before swooping back to perch.

The Little Owl can sit still for hours, a round ball of fluff, but if alarmed, it can suddenly go very thin as it stretches upwards.

White eyebrows and piercing yellow eyes give this tiny owl a fierce expression. Look for it at dusk in hedgerows and by the sides of country roads.

TAWNY OWL *Strix aluco*

38CM, 15IN

Arguably the most widespread of the British owls (although it is absent from Ireland), but one of the most difficult to see. By day, Tawny Owls roost in holes or in trees, when their presence may be betrayed by the noise of small birds mobbing them. Even then it may be hard to spot the owl unless it flies, and even when it does, it will soon glide away into the woods and be lost again. Otherwise, you may see the silhouette of a bird at night when it is out hunting. It is rarely far from woods with mature trees. Tawny Owl is basically brown and streaky. It shares this type of plumage with several other species, but Tawny is considerably larger than Little Owl and would rarely be seen in open country like Short-eared Owl. It is most likely to be confused with Long-eared Owl (see page 140). Tawny is plumper, rounder faced and lacks any ear tufts. The call is the familiar 'hoo hoo hooo', and a sharp 'keewick'.

A woodland bird and very nocturnal in its habits, the Tawny Owl is much more likely to be heard than seen. Feeds mainly on small mammals such as Wood Mice.

By day the Tawny Owl roosts, often hunched against a tree trunk, when despite its camouflage its presence may be advertised by small birds mobbing it.

Juveniles (right). When still by no means fully fledged, the young may start to scramble about among the branches. Tawny Owls nest in holes in trees.

LONG-EARED OWL *Asio otus*

36CM, 14IN

Not an easy bird to see, although it breeds quite widely throughout Britain, mainly in conifer plantations. The most common owl in Ireland (where it is also found in deciduous woods). Very secretive during the breeding season, but you may hear its low, long hoot, or the high-pitched 'squeaky gate' calls of youngsters. Your best chance of seeing Long-eared Owl is if you visit a winter roost. This may be in quite open bramble or bushes, and may contain up to a dozen birds, which sit beautifully camouflaged, defying you to count them. These are probably immigrants from the Continent, and in late autumn they sometimes arrive on the coasts along with Short-eared Owls. The ear tufts are only visible if you get a good view of a bird at rest, when it can be seen that they are clearly much longer than those of Short-eared. Tawny Owl (see page 139) is plumper and rounder faced, has no ear tufts at all, and has darker eyes compared with the bright orange of Long-eared.

Generally most day-flying large brown owls will be Short-eared. Long-eared tends to roost by day, exquisitely camouflaged beside a tree trunk.

Compared with Short-eared, note more extensive streaking on the underparts (breast only on Short-eared) and slightly more rufous patches on upperwing. Longer and slimmer than Tawny Owl.

SHORT-EARED OWL *Asio flammeus*

38CM, 15IN

Quite commonly hunts during daylight, so it's a good rule that any day-hunting large brown owl is likely to be Short-eared. Quarters open country, flapping and gliding with wings held in a shallow 'V', at a distance very reminiscent of a harrier and – since female and juvenile harriers are also largely brown – look for the ring tail and slimmer build of Hen and Montagu's Harriers (see pages 63 and 64). Breeds in moorland and young plantations in northern Britain, but you are most likely to see Short-eared Owls on passage in late autumn, or at their wintering places, flat, rough ground or marsh land. In flight, very similar to Long-eared Owl, but streaking on the underparts is across the breast only, and contrasts with the whiter belly and flanks. The upperwing has yellowy – rather than rufous – wing patches, but this is variable and hard to see. Often perches on the ground or on very low stumps or tussocks. Song – only heard in its northern breeding haunts – is a hollow 'boo boo boo boo'.

Compared with Long-eared the streaking on the underparts is across the breast only and contrasts with the whiter belly and flanks. Upperwing has yellowy rather than rufous patches.

At rest, the face is rounder than Long-eared's, eyes yellower and ear tufts almost invisible.

EUROPEAN NIGHTJAR *Caprimulgus europaeus*

27CM, 10.5IN

Extremely difficult to see. A summer visitor (arriving in mid-May and rarely seen after the breeding season). Breeds on heathlands and low plantations, mainly in the south and east of England. You are not likely to find a European Nightjar unless you visit one of its known sites, preferably in late May or early June. Then wait until dusk, when the birds will begin churring – the noise sounds rather like a distant motor scooter. Look towards the lightest part of the sky and hope that the bird flies through it, chasing insects, giving a soft, sharp 'too wick' call. You may see white flashes on the wing tips and tail end, but generally the plumage is as dense as 'dead leaves'. Although European Nightjars are long-distance migrants (they winter in Africa) they are very rarely seen on passage. Perhaps the species most often misidentified as European Nightjar is Mistle Thrush, especially the speckly young birds, which also have white tail edges and a rattling call. However, Mistle Thrushes are much more common and only fly by day.

Flight shape is slim, long-winged and long-tailed, and acrobatic – very much like that of an agile, nocturnal falcon. Male shows most conspicuous white flashes on wing tips and tail end.

Plumage as dense as 'dead leaves'. This is precisely why the bird is so utterly camouflaged on the ground on its nest, or roosting along a tree branch.

COMMON SWIFT *Apus apus*

16.5CM, 6.5IN

Often seen flying with swallows and martins (see pages 165–7). Swifts are summer visitors, one of the latest to arrive – usually in very late April, more commonly in May – and one of the earliest to leave, being rarely seen in numbers after early August. Compared with swallows and martins, they are larger, with narrow, crescent-shaped wings and a forked tail, often held closed. A flying sickle! The plumage looks all black, though there is a small pale patch on the throat, more conspicuous in young birds. The call also draws attention: a high-pitched 'screaming', particularly noisy when birds first arrive and chase around in parties displaying. The diet of swifts consists wholly of insects caught on the wing; these are in abundance in warm summer weather. They are seen feeding over built-up areas, open country and fresh water. Swifts never perch on wires and are usually only seen to land as they disappear into their nests under eaves.

A really remarkable bird, the Common Swift spends most of its life flying. Watch the birds spiralling up into the sky on a calm evening to sleep on the wing.

Adults. Common Swift roosts only when nesting and may fly more than 1 million miles in its lifetime. Juveniles leave the nest, flying south without their parents, and may remain on the wing for two years.

KINGFISHER *Alcedo atthis*

16.5CM, 6.5IN

Arguably Britain's most beautiful and most easily recognized bird. Found near lakes, rivers and canals all over Britain, except Scotland, where it is restricted to the south. Seen perched, it is unmistakable, but it is perhaps more often seen flashing past and disappearing around a corner. In flight, it can look either metallic blue or bright orange, depending which side catches the light. The call is a short 'peep peep', and it is often this noise that attracts attention before you actually see the bird. Once perched in cover alongside water, Kingfishers can be very hard to spot, despite their brilliant colours. The best technique is often to scan along likely looking perches with binoculars. Kingfishers nest deep in tunnels excavated into a sandy river bank. The female has a reddish base to the beak. In winter, birds may move to coastal estuaries, and they are sometimes even seen on rocks and breakwaters at the seaside. Kingfishers hunt for food by diving, usually from a perch, but may hover briefly. Prey is swallowed head first.

Dives like an arrow to catch fish in its long, dagger-like beak. Usually fishes from a perch, but sometimes hovers above the water before plunging down.

A flash of metallic blue or bright orange, depending on what catches the light, is the best view most of us get of a Kingfisher.

Juveniles (above) must learn to fish quickly or they will starve. Kingfishers are usually double-brooded, enabling populations to recover quickly after hard winters, when many die.

Adult. Short-tailed and dumpy, Kingfishers are perhaps surprisingly small – smaller than a Starling. They sit on small overhanging branches staring intently into the water below.

144

GREEN WOODPECKER *Picus viridis*

32CM, 12.5IN

The largest British woodpecker. Widespread in wood and parkland, though scarcer in Scotland (but increasing) and absent from Ireland. Frequently seen on the ground – including on lawns and in dunes – where it hunts for ants and hops along rather clumsily. Using its strong bill and long tongue it explores the galleries deep in an ant hill, extracting ants and pupae. The olive-green plumage is quite different from the plumages of other British woodpeckers. When it flies, it flashes a yellow rump, which has often lead to claims of Golden Oriole (see page 234). Green Woodpeckers drum less often than the other species, but draw attention to themselves by their noisy laughing call (its colloquial name is 'yaffle'). Juveniles are heavily streaked and barred on the underparts and have less vivid red heads than adults.

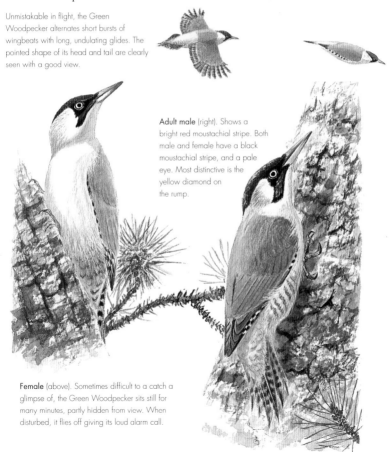

Unmistakable in flight, the Green Woodpecker alternates short bursts of wingbeats with long, undulating glides. The pointed shape of its head and tail are clearly seen with a good view.

Adult male (right). Shows a bright red moustachial stripe. Both male and female have a black moustachial stripe, and a pale eye. Most distinctive is the yellow diamond on the rump.

Female (above). Sometimes difficult to a catch a glimpse of, the Green Woodpecker sits still for many minutes, partly hidden from view. When disturbed, it flies off giving its loud alarm call.

GREAT SPOTTED WOODPECKER *Dendrocopos major*

23CM, 9IN

Widespread in British woodlands but absent in Ireland. The larger and more common of the two spotted woodpeckers. Not uncommon in gardens, even feeding on nut bags. Compared with Lesser Spotted, Great is clearly larger and has conspicuous white shoulder patches on either side of a black back (Lesser Spotted is finely barred in this area). The call is a short liquid 'tchik', which becomes more varied and bubbly when birds are breeding and displaying. They drum loudly in spring (beginning in February). Both sexes have red undertails. The male has a red nape, distinguishing it clearly from the female, and the juvenile has a red crown (although this disappears in autumn when the bird moults). The flight is undulating, the bird regularly closing its wings and dropping before flapping again; this style is typical of woodpeckers.

Juvenile (left). The stump of a dead birch tree is actually a favourite site to excavate a nest cavity, which may take two weeks to complete. Easy to locate when the young are noisy.

Female (above) and male (right) breeding plumage. Dead and dying trees are a good source of food; the birds extract insects and larvae with their strong bills.

In flight (left) the bird can be clearly identified by its large white shoulder patches and bright red undertail.

146

LESSER SPOTTED WOODPECKER *Dendrocopos minor*

14.5CM, 5.75IN

Less common than Great Spotted. Found in southern England and Wales, but absent further north and in Ireland. Lesser Spotted really is tiny – the size of a House Sparrow. Its drumming and singing in early spring often draw attention to its presence. The call is a high-pitched 'kikikiki' (not unlike that of a speeded-up Kestrel). Compared with Great Spotted, Lesser is clearly smaller and has fine barring over the back and closed wings (Great Spotted has large white shoulder patches). The male has a red crown, the female a pale one. The flight is typical undulating woodpecker style, but – because of the bird's small size – this often doesn't immediately catch the eye. Look for it high in the tree canopy where it likes to feed. With practice, it is possible to distinguish the longer, more high-pitched drumming of Lesser Spotted compared with Great's. Likewise, a practised eye can distinguish between the different-sized nest holes of woodpecker species. Lessers rarely visit gardens, preferring woods and parkland.

Juvenile (right) has a red crown. Lesser Spotteds are distinguished by the fine black-and-white barring across the back and wings.

Male (below). Recognizable by his striking red crown. Both birds excavate the nest cavity, which is often on the underside of a dead branch and usually hard to find.

Female breeding plumage (below). Nest holes are found at every level among the trees, from a few feet above ground to over 21m (70ft) high in the branches.

GREAT GREY SHRIKE *Lanius excubitor*

24CM, 9.5IN

The other 'regular' shrike in Britain (see Red-backed Shrike, page 234), but in fact a pretty rare bird. A few migrants appear – mainly in October and November and occasionally in May – and a small number winter from Europe, usually on heathlands mainly in the south and east. Larger than Red-backed Shrike. Pale grey above, white below and with a black mask, with white wing flashes in flight and a long tail with white edges. The sexes look similar, though female and juvenile have faint grey bars on breast. Like all shrikes, tends to perch on wires and tops of bushes, and can be very conspicuous, constantly flicking its tail. Despite this, it is perfectly possible to wander a heathland all day without seeing a Great Grey that you know is there somewhere. Shrikes are famous for their unsavoury habits of impaling prey on thorns, saving it in a 'larder' to eat later. The Great Grey is large enough to take small birds and mammals, as well as insects.

Lengthy flights tend to be undulating: short ones between perches are generally low to the ground, sweeping upwards at the last moment.

Male (below). Upright stance is typical, together with tail continually flicking up and down, as it watches and waits for prey such as a mouse, which it catches by a downwards swoop.

Female (above). Slightly hooked bill betrays the shrike's predatory habits. A bird of heathland, it perches on conspicuous posts, but may be very difficult to catch sight of.

MAGPIE *Pica pica*

46CM, 18IN

A very familiar bird and becoming even more so, as numbers appear to be increasing, though it is still scarce in northern Scotland. Because it takes nestlings and eggs – and is very conspicuous when doing so – it has become the target of some distrust, not to say dislike. However, there is little evidence that Magpies are seriously depleting the numbers of British songbirds. The decline in certain species is far more to do with habitat loss, pesticides and so on (not to mention cats). Magpies are in fact very intelligent and handsome birds, their pied plumage having a metallic gloss. They are also pretty unmistakable. Their call is a chattering 'chack chacking'. They build large, domed nests made out of twigs towards the tops of trees. Out of the breeding season they are often seen in parties – sometimes known as Magpie weddings – and even larger numbers may gather at winter roosts. Nest is large and football shaped.

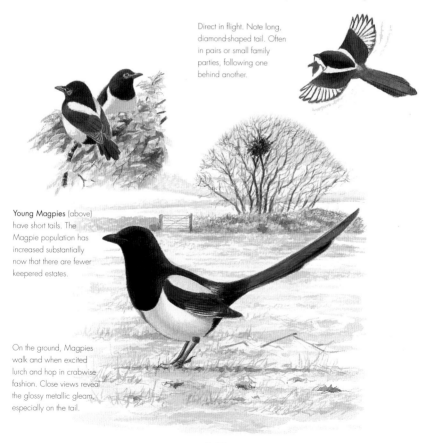

Direct in flight. Note long, diamond-shaped tail. Often in pairs or small family parties, following one behind another.

Young Magpies (above) have short tails. The Magpie population has increased substantially now that there are fewer keepered estates.

On the ground, Magpies walk and when excited lurch and hop in crabwise fashion. Close views reveal the glossy metallic gleam, especially on the tail.

JAY *Garrulus glandarius*

34CM, 13.5IN

A familiar bird to most people, yet one that is often the cause of confusion, or at least surprise. Resident in many parts of Britain, and often visits parks and gardens. However, its habits are fairly secretive, and therefore its vivid colours often seem to cause a bit of a shock. Reports of rare and exotic birds often turn out to be just Jays. Different bits of this undeniably handsome bird seem to catch different eyes – the crest, the blue flash on the wing, or the vivid white rump when it flies and, of course, the salmon-pink body, which can look very bright in sunlight. The flight style is rather bounding, on rounded wings. The only species with which it is really confusable is the rare Hoopoe (see page 231) which is also pink, black and white, but very distinctive.

White rump, black tail and blue-and-white wing flashes make an encounter with a Jay quite startling. Jays enjoy bathing; puddles on a road may tempt one into the open.

Jays make a ghastly noise: a harsh screeching that invariably panics all the other birds in the garden – with good reason, since Jays readily feed on nestlings and eggs.

In autumn Jays turn to acorns. They eat some, bury a lot more, presumably for later, and are reckoned to be important agents in the spread of oak trees.

150

JACKDAW *Corvus monedula*

33CM, 13IN

Considerably smaller than Rook or Carrion Crow, and with a largely grey head, contrasting with the sooty black of the rest of the bird. The white eye is set off by a darker face. Breeds widely in Britain, but is absent or scarce in some areas. Colonies often favour old ruins, quarries and sea cliffs, as well as old and dead trees, and also church towers, and even down disused chimneys. In certain areas the Jackdaw is a familiar sight in towns, whereas the other black crows are much more 'country' birds. The call is a short 'chack' (from which it gets its name), and a slightly more echoey 'keeow'. The most similar species is the rare Chough (see page 235). A close-up view will soon reveal the differences, but they can also be distinguished in flight by the Chough's more ragged-looking wing tips, and its higher pitched, more sneezing call. Jackdaws often join other crows (corvids) in mixed feeding flocks in winter.

White eye, and grey head and nape, contrast with sooty plumage. Jackdaw walks with quick, jaunty strides, less sedate than either Carrion Crow or Rook. Also flies faster, with quicker wingbeats.

Jackdaws nest in holes in ruins, quarries and old tree trunks – that's why they often find chimneys make very convenient nest sites.

151

RAVEN *Corvus corax*

64CM, 25IN

The largest of the black crows by far, but this isn't always immediately appreciated unless other species are present for comparison. Ravens are found only in western Britain and Ireland, and only near sea cliffs and upland craggy areas, though they will feed on farmland and even refuse tips. They build nests of sticks and twigs on cliffs and crags, and sometimes in trees. The Raven's head is particularly large, with a big, deep bill and a shaggy throat. In flight, its tail is noticeably wedge-shaped, wings often with primaries spread into open 'fingers'. Ravens are most often seen singly, in pairs or in small parties – but they do gather in larger groups at roost, although not in the large flocks of Carrion Crow or Rook. Pairs often tumble and roll in mid-air during their display flight. They are very agile in the air and seem to enjoy playing in the wind. Imposing even at a distance, Ravens have a very gruff, deep croaking call.

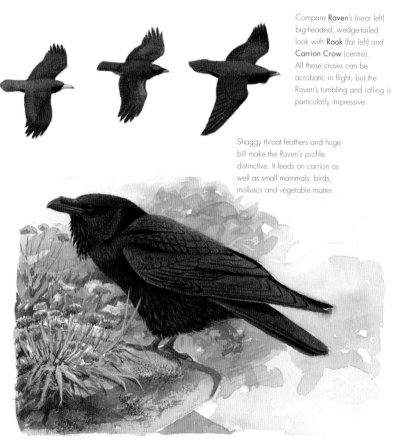

Compare **Raven**'s (near left) big-headed, wedge-tailed look with **Rook** (far left) and **Carrion Crow** (centre). All these crows can be acrobatic in flight, but the Raven's tumbling and rolling is particularly impressive.

Shaggy throat feathers and huge bill make the Raven's profile distinctive. It feeds on carrion as well as small mammals, birds, molluscs and vegetable matter.

ROOK *Corvus frugilegus*

46CM, 18IN

Breeds throughout Britain, always in colonies, known of course as rookeries. The nests are conspicuous, built in the tops of tall trees. Otherwise feeds on farmland, and rarely comes into truly built-up areas. Very similar to Carrion Crow, but Rook is slightly smaller and less stockily built, the crown of its head is noticeably peaked, and its bill is more dagger-shaped and whitish (though young Rooks have dark bills). The feathering at the tops of the legs is also shaggier, like a pair of feathery shorts. The flight silhouette is subtly different from a Carrion Crow's, with slimmer wings, a slightly longer, more rounded tail and faster wingbeats. The call is 'caar', less croaky and more echoey than a Carrion Crow's. Feeds much more on grain and vegetable matter than Carrion Crow, but also takes invertebrates, small mammals and carrion. Often feeds in flocks, sometimes very large ones.

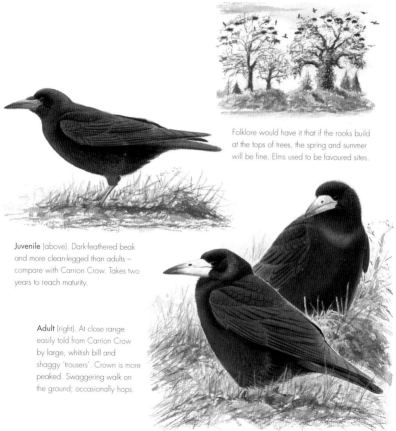

Folklore would have it that if the rooks build at the tops of trees, the spring and summer will be fine. Elms used to be favoured sites.

Juvenile (above). Dark-feathered beak and more clean-legged than adults – compare with Carrion Crow. Takes two years to reach maturity.

Adult (right). At close range easily told from Carrion Crow by large, whitish bill and shaggy 'trousers'. Crown is more peaked. Swaggering walk on the ground; occasionally hops.

CARRION CROW *Corvus corone*
HOODED CROW *Corvus cornis*

47CM, 18.5IN

There are five species of black 'crow' in Britain. **Carrion Crows** are found throughout the British Isles, but are replaced in Ireland, northern and western Scotland and the Isle of Man by the species known as **Hooded Crow**. This is in fact very easy to recognize, with its grey body, and black hood and wings. Carrion Crow (the all-black species) is most similar to Raven and Rook (see pages 152 and 153), but Raven is much bigger and Rook has a white bill and steeper forehead. It used to be said that if you saw a flock of crows in a field, they were Rooks, but this doesn't really make sense. Crows can gather in large, winter-feeding flocks and at roosts. However, they do not breed in colonies like Rooks. Their call is a croaking 'craw', but they also produce variations, some of which sound strangely hollow, almost comical. They are common in town parks, where Rooks would rarely wander. They nest in trees, and also on cliff ledges.

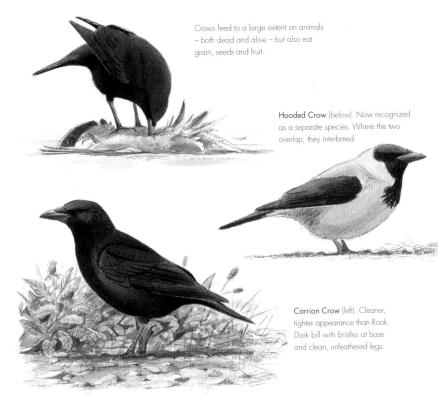

Crows feed to a large extent on animals – both dead and alive – but also eat grain, seeds and fruit.

Hooded Crow (below). Now recognized as a separate species. Where the two overlap, they interbreed.

Carrion Crow (left). Cleaner, tighter appearance than Rook. Dark bill with bristles at base and clean, unfeathered legs.

FIRECREST *Regulus ignicapilla*

9CM, 3.5IN

Scarce in Britain, most frequently seen on migration – mainly at coastal locations in the south and east – but small numbers also breed in the south. Prefers mature conifers close to mixed woodlands. Looks slightly bigger than Goldcrest, probably because of its more streamlined face pattern. The white stripe over the eye is the most conspicuous feature. The upperparts are greener than Goldcrest's and the underparts cleaner white. There is also a quite striking golden suffusion on the shoulder.

Males (near right) have fireier crests than **females** (bottom, right). **Juveniles** (top, right) have no crests. Call: similar to Goldcrest's though a little rougher. Song: an evenly repeated note, accelerating on same pitch, lacking Goldcrest's trill. Note the vivid white eyebrow.

GOLDCREST *Regulus regulus*

9CM, 3.5IN

Our tiniest bird, found all over Britain. Breeds in conifers but in winter visits all kinds of woods and hedgerows, and gardens. Numbers are considerably swollen by continental immigrants and – especially in October – large 'falls' may occur, especially on the east coast. Dark-edged wing bar is as conspicuous as crest on crown. This has an orange centre on the male, yellow on female, and is lacking in very young birds, which are most likely to be mistaken for warblers.

Male (left). Goldcrests often dangle under leaves or hover when feeding. They frequently join roving tit flocks in winter. Can look like a very small warbler, but note wing bar.

Female (right). The call is a soft, repeated 'seeseesee'. The song repeats two thin notes on a rising scale and finishes with a trill.

BLUE TIT *Cyanistes caeruleus*

11.5CM, 4.5IN

Well known and well loved. A widespread breeding bird all over Britain, which often uses nest boxes, as well as holes and crevices in just about anything. Very familiar in gardens, where it readily comes to bird tables and ingenious feeding contraptions, as well as removing putty from window fixings. No other bird has its blue crown, and white face with black eyeline look. Juveniles are duller than adults, with a yellow wash on the face. They are extremely active and agile in pursuit of food, especially when they are feeding their broods, which can number ten or more. Mortality is high, but the large families (up to 14 eggs are laid) result in the species surviving at a healthy level, and numbers soon build up after a harsh winter. The call is a thin 'see see' (less rhythmic than either Goldcrest's or Long-tailed Tit's) and the song is similarly sibilant and includes a trembly little trill.

Adults (below). Bright blue crown and white face with black eyestripe. As is the case with other tit species the sexes are alike, but with both at the bird table you might notice a difference in brightness.

Juveniles (above). Duller than the adults, the white on the face being replaced by a yellow wash. Tits usually rear only one brood per year, but make it a large one.

156

GREAT TIT *Parus major*

14CM, 5.5IN

Almost as familiar as Blue Tit, but absent or scarce in the Highlands of Scotland and the Northern Isles. Nearly as big as a House Sparrow, and perhaps even more aggressive. Often chases other tits off feeders. The most obvious features are the white cheeks on an otherwise shiny black head, and the black stripe down the yellow chest (broader in males than females). The most similar species is Coal Tit (see page 160), which also has white cheeks, as well as a white nape (back of the neck); it is fawn below and considerably smaller. Great Tits make all sorts of noises, some of them very loud and sounding almost electronic. These include a sharp 'chink chink' and a repeated 'teecher teecher'. Great Tit's repertoire is so diverse that birdwatchers often say that if they can't recognize a woodland call, it's probably a Great Tit. Nests in holes and nest boxes.

Young (left). Duller and more washed out than adults.

Female (far right). Feeds on beechmast in winter. In a good mast year, many survive the winter; in poor years many die.

Male. Can be distinguished from female by broad black band extending the length of the belly. Like Blue Tit, a frequent winter visitor to bird tables.

MARSH TIT *Poecile palustris*

11.5CM, 4.5IN

Marsh and Willow Tit are extremely similar, so much so that even expert birdwatchers sometimes confuse them. Both are resident in woods in England, Wales and southern Scotland. Neither is exclusively dependent on the wet habitat implied by its name. In fact, Marsh Tit in particular may occur in drier areas. It very rarely visit gardens, and is an unusual visitor to bird tables. Compared with Willow, Marsh Tit is slightly less bull-necked, and has a glossy black cap (dull in Willow) and a smaller black bib. Juveniles have a dull sooty black cap like Willow's. Marsh Tit's most distinctive call is an explosive 'pitchoo'. Other buzzier scolding calls are more difficult to distinguish from Willow Tit's. Both Marsh and Willow lack the white nape and wing bars of Coal Tit (see page 160). Nests in holes in trees. Feeds on insects and seeds, especially beechmast.

Usually rears a single brood in a hole in a tree such as birch or alder. Strongly territorial and aggressive.

Shiny black cap and less bull-necked appearance best distinguish it from Willow Tit.

Note neat black bib. Willow's is a bit bigger. Wing uniform, lacking pale patch of Willow Tit.

158

WILLOW TIT *Poecile montanus*

11.5CM, 4.5IN

Very similar to Marsh Tit. In fact, Willow was not differentiated from Marsh Tit in Britain until the beginning of the 20th century. Resident in damp woodlands in England, Wales and southern Scotland. Unlike Marsh Tit, it excavates its own nest holes, which is probably why it prefers damper areas with rotting wood. The plumage is very similar to Marsh Tit's, but Willow Tit is slightly more bull-necked, the black crown is dull (not shiny), the black bib is a little larger and there is often (but not always) a frosty pale patch on the closed wing. The most characteristic call is a nasal repeated 'chair chair'. Other buzzy calls are less easy to separate from Marsh Tit's. Both Willow and Marsh Tit lack the white nape and wing bars of Coal Tit. Note also that male Blackcap (page 175) is basically brownish with a black cap, but is larger, slower in its movements, and lacks white cheeks and a black bib.

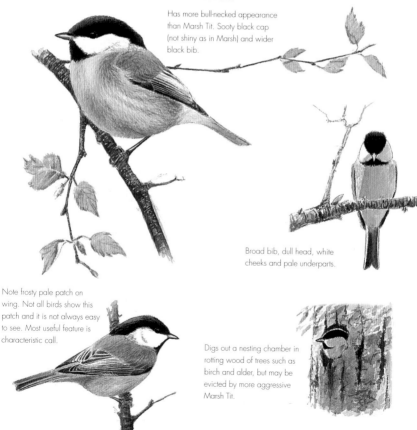

Has more bull-necked appearance than Marsh Tit. Sooty black cap (not shiny as in Marsh) and wider black bib.

Broad bib, dull head, white cheeks and pale underparts.

Note frosty pale patch on wing. Not all birds show this patch and it is not always easy to see. Most useful feature is characteristic call.

Digs out a nesting chamber in rotting wood of trees such as birch and alder, but may be evicted by more aggressive Marsh Tit.

159

COAL TIT *Periparus ater*

11.5CM, 4.5IN

A widespread breeding bird found more in conifers than the other common tit species, but occurs in broadleaved woodland too. Also joins roving tit flocks out of the breeding season, and will visit garden feeders. However, it seems much shyer than Blue and Great Tits, often nipping in, grabbing a peanut and dashing away, probably to store it somewhere. For this reason, it may seem scarcer than it really is. Small and neat (slightly smaller than Blue Tit). It has white cheeks on a black head – a bit like a Great Tit's – and also has a white nape (back of neck). The underparts vary from buffish to off-white. The whitish areas are yellower in juveniles than in adults. The call is a shrill 'tsuueee', and the song a high-pitched, repeated 'teechu teechu teechu'. Both Marsh and Willow Tit have a rather similar fawn-bodied, black-headed look, but neither has the white nape or extended black chinstrap. They also lack the Coal Tit's white wing bars.

Adult (right). Coal Tits in Ireland have a yellowy wash on the cheeks and nape, with buffier upperparts and a yellower flush to the underparts.

Broad white stripe at nape makes an **adult** Coal Tit look like a little Mohican! White wing bars help to separate it quickly from Marsh and Willow Tits.

Juvenile (below). Colours are more subdued than those of an adult.

160

BEARDED TIT *Panurus biarmicus*

16.5CM, 6.5IN

Found only in reedbeds, mainly in East Anglia and the south-east. Its alternative – and better – name is Bearded Reedling. Plump-bodied and long-tailed, nothing else with this shape lives in reedbeds. Both sexes are a rich orangey above, with blackish marks on the wings, but the male has a wonderful powder-blue head and smart black moustaches. Unfortunately, this isn't an easy bird to get a good view of. Bearded Tits usually betray their presence by calling: a ringing 'ching ching' like tiny bells. They sometimes then flit rather feebly across the reed tops, before quickly flopping back into cover. Your best bet is to watch a channel between the reeds on a calm day, and wait for birds to make the crossing. They will sometimes shin up the reeds, and look around before they flutter across. In some winters small parties of birds wander to smaller reedbeds, away from the usual breeding haunts, but they are never common. Most of their strongholds are at well-known bird reserves.

Short flights on whirring wings. Bearded Tits do not like to fly far. Watch a channel between the reeds and wait.

Juvenile (below). Streakier than both male and female, with dark outer tail feathers.

Male (right). Has no beard – why isn't it called Moustached Tit? Shuffles up and down reed stems, feeding on insects, but also eats reed seeds in winter. Listen for 'ching ching' call.

Female (above, left). Shares the male's basic orange colour, even if it isn't so intense, and lacks the moustaches.

161

WOODLARK *Lullula arborea*

15CM, 6IN

A rather scarce breeding bird, in very specific type of habitat: not strictly speaking woods. It prefers heath or downland with scattered trees, and is particularly fond of recently cleared areas, usually near or among conifers. Breeds in southern England and parts of Wales only. These are areas also frequented by Skylarks, so careful identification is required. Woodlark is slightly smaller. The face and head have a much stronger pattern, with a conspicuous pale stripe over the eye, joining at the back of the neck; more clearly defined cheek, with a rusty interior, and a small – but surprisingly obvious – black-and-white 'notch' at the shoulder of the closed wing. The call is a rather lovely fluty 'tit loo eeet'; the song is sweeter and less frantic than Skylark's, often heard at dawn before it is even light. Scarce away from its breeding haunts, but single birds are occasionally seen on passage, usually in October or November.

The wings have no white trailing edges, and the tail has white only at the tip. This gives Woodlark a plainer overall look than that of a Skylark when it flies.

Adult spring plumage. On the ground, Woodlark gives a clear view of the characteristic black-and-white wing 'notch' and pale stripe over the eye.

SHORELARK *Eremophila alpestris*

16.5CM, 6.5IN

A rare bird that occurs in small flocks, mainly on the east coast in late autumn and winter. It does indeed feed almost exclusively on shingly shores or on nearby saltmarshes, but Skylarks also occur in the same habitat, and usually in much larger numbers. Slightly smaller than Skylark, and a shade paler brown and less scaly on the upperparts. The most obvious feature is the face pattern, which – on the male – is yellow, with black on forehead, cheeks and breast. As it attains breeding plumage it develops two small black 'horns'. This pattern is much fainter in females and young birds, but is always noticeable and distinctive. In flight, it shows white outer tail feathers, but no white trailing edge. The call is a thin 'tsee ree' (thinner than Skylark's buzzy squeak call). Winter flocks tend to be faithful to the same area until they leave in spring.

A winter flock of Shorelarks characterized by their undulating flight. A scarce bird seen mainly on the east coast, where it feeds along the shoreline and in nearby saltmarshes and dunes.

Female (above) and **male in breeding plumage** (right). The bright yellow of the male is duller in winter. Shorelarks walk and run along the ground in search of food.

SKYLARK *Alauda arvensis*

18CM, 7IN

Widespread breeding bird found in more or less all treeless habitats, except the very tops of mountains. Most easily identified by its effusive song, which is delivered from way up in the sky before it closes its wings, drops into cover, then walks to its nest (i.e. it doesn't drop onto the nest). Skylarks are also migrants, and considerable movements, especially in late autumn, involve both British birds and continental immigrants. Individual migrants are the birds most likely to cause identification puzzles, as they are similar to other lark species and pipits. Skylark is rather bulky and tends to shuffle along, crouched quite low to the ground when feeding. It has conspicuous white outer tail feathers, but this is a feature shown by several other streaky little brown birds, for example pipits and female buntings. Skylark's call is also distinctive: a slightly bubbly 'prrp prrp'. Birds in winter sometimes make an odd short, squeaky call, which can be puzzling at first. For detailed differences from Woodlark and Shorelark, see pages 162 and 163. A good general point is that Skylark has the plainest face.

Skylark shows its most unique feature when it flies – a white trailing edge to its wings found in no other British lark. Its song flight can last up to five minutes.

Winter. When they are not singing, Skylarks spend their time on the ground. They sometimes form quite large flocks in winter, usually on stubble or freshly disturbed fields.

Summer plumage. When disturbed, Skylark tends to crouch rather than run. Crest not always obvious. It is usually seen when a bird is excited or alarmed.

164

SWALLOW *Hirundo rustica*

18–20CM, 7–7.5IN

Swallow and martins belong to a family called hirundines (*hirondelle* is the French for swallow). There are three common British species (see also Sand and House Martins, pages 166 and 167). All are summer visitors. Swallows differ from martins in having longer wings and tail streamers, and a red throat above a bluish breast band. At rest, they are easily identified. In flight, Swallow looks more streamlined and shows an all-dark head. Common Swift is larger, with crescent-shaped wings, and looks completely black (see page 143). Young birds have short streamers, and the red on the face is a more washed-out dull pink. Swallows nest is an open mud cup, usually on a beam of a barn or outhouse, and they often return to the same site year after year. Large numbers roost in reedbeds in the autumn before migrating. The call is a twittery 'tswit', the song an excitable longer version with a similarly twittery character.

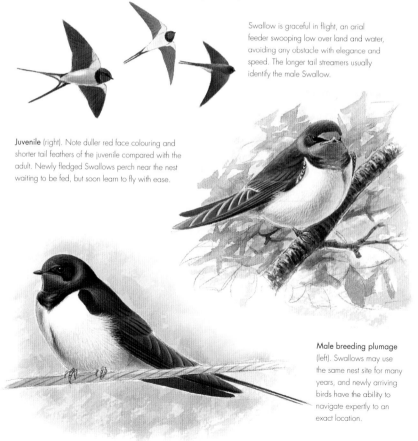

Swallow is graceful in flight, an arial feeder swooping low over land and water, avoiding any obstacle with elegance and speed. The longer tail streamers usually identify the male Swallow.

Juvenile (right). Note duller red face colouring and shorter tail feathers of the juvenile compared with the adult. Newly fledged Swallows perch near the nest waiting to be fed, but soon learn to fly with ease.

Male breeding plumage (left). Swallows may use the same nest site for many years, and newly arriving birds have the ability to navigate expertly to an exact location.

SAND MARTIN *Riparia riparia*

12CM, 4.75IN

The smallest and 'feeblest' of the hirundines (swallow family), with a rather weak, fluttery flight. The upperparts are sandy-brown and the underparts white, but with a narrow brown breast band. In flight the species lacks the darkness of either Swallow or House Martin, and has no white rump or tail streamers. Sand Martins are one of the first migrants to arrive, often in early March in southern counties, but they rarely linger long into September. Migrants at both ends of the season often gather over lakes and reservoirs, where they mix with other hirundines in their search for insects. Sand Martins nest in burrows in 'traditional' colonies in river banks, sea cliffs and quarries. They excavate burrows at least 1m (3ft) deep, and may remove stones several times their own weight. Some years ago numbers dropped considerably, probably due to droughts in Africa, but recent years have seen a recovery. Found all over Britain, and particularly numerous along Scottish rivers. Call is a dry 'tchrrup', clearly different from House Martin's call, also incorporated into its chattery song.

On the wing, Sand Martin is easily distinguished from other hirundines by its shorter and only slightly forked tail. Its call is harsher than the Swallow or House Martin's.

Sand Martins are gregarious birds, nesting in colonies and clinging to the banks containing their nests. Outside the breeding season, before migrating they roost socially, particularly in reedbeds.

Upperparts sandy-brown, underparts white with narrow brown breast band. The smallest of the swallow family.

HOUSE MARTIN *Delichon urbica*

12.5CM, 5IN

A summer visitor, usually arriving a few days later than Swallow and often lingering later in the autumn. Most easily separated from Swallow in flight, by its pure white rump. Otherwise, the upperparts are velvety black (compared with bluish-black in Swallow and sandy-brown in Sand Martin) and the underparts pure white. An unusual feature, sometimes seen when a House Martin is perched or clinging by the nest, is the short legs and feet, which have tiny white feathers even on the toes. The flight style is just a little less graceful than a Swallow's, with broader based wings, and House Martins often fly higher when hunting insects. The tail is forked, but with no streamers. House Martins build mud-ball nests under the guttering of buildings, often in large colonies. Before there were buildings they presumably nested on cliffs. However, sadly and mysteriously, many of these colonies appear to be dwindling in recent years. The call is a cheerful 'chirrupping', also incorporated into the more twittery song. Found all over Britain, but scarcer in the far north.

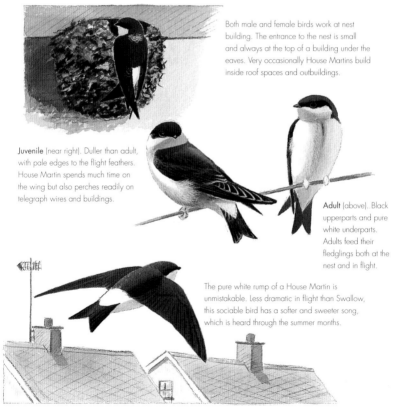

Both male and female birds work at nest building. The entrance to the nest is small and always at the top of a building under the eaves. Very occasionally House Martins build inside roof spaces and outbuildings.

Juvenile (near right). Duller than adult, with pale edges to the flight feathers. House Martin spends much time on the wing but also perches readily on telegraph wires and buildings.

Adult (above). Black upperparts and pure white underparts. Adults feed their fledglings both at the nest and in flight.

The pure white rump of a House Martin is unmistakable. Less dramatic in flight than Swallow, this sociable bird has a softer and sweeter song, which is heard through the summer months.

LONG-TAILED TIT *Aegithalos caudatus*

14CM, 5.5IN

An exquisite little bird with a dumpy little body and very long tail. The plumage is pink, black and white, and it really can't be mistaken for anything else. The Long-tailed Tit builds lovely little lichen-ball nests woven together with spider's webs (which give a nest a wonderful elastic quality to house a growing brood of up to 12 chicks). The birds breed deep in hedges and low cover in most parts of Britain. Out of the breeding season they often visit gardens, but rarely come onto the nut bags so beloved of other tits. They are frequently seen in parties: usually half a dozen or so, but sometimes many more, especially if they are with other tits. It's a pretty safe rule that if you see one Long-tailed Tit, others will soon follow. The call is a high-pitched 'see see see', similar to a Goldcrest's call, but on a slightly lower pitch, and they also make other low, short trilling sounds. The juveniles have dingier heads than adults.

Almost always in family parties: if you see one, look for more. Feeds mainly on insects, and also seeds and buds, but not really a bird-table bird.

Pink lollipop birds – Long-tailed Tits teeter and swing on twigs, toppling slowly over like one of those balancing acrobat toys.

Pink, black and white plumage with that long tail is unmistakable. It looks rather like a mobile powder puff. Juveniles have dingier heads.

WOOD WARBLER *Phylloscopus sibilatrix*

12.5CM, 5IN

As the name implies, belongs to the group of warblers that inhabit woodlands rather than scrub or reeds. This applies to breeding preferences, as all warblers can turn up in pretty odd – and sometimes quite treeless – places on migration. Wood Warblers need mature woodland, especially with oak and beech. Their distribution is curiously patchy in Britain: scarce in south-east England, northern Scotland and Ireland, yet surprisingly common in some of the Western Isles. Wood Warbler is the most distinctive of the three common British wood-loving warblers. The best feature is the lemon-yellow breast, contrasting with the silky white belly and undertail. The upperparts are a bright green, and there is a conspicuous yellow stripe over the eye. The wings are particularly long, giving the bird a short-tailed look that is quite striking when seen from below. The song is most often a single wispy note repeated until it becomes a trembling sibilant trill. This is appropriately accompanied by a similarly trembling movement of the bird's whole body. The call is a loud 'pee–u pee–u'.

Long wings give the bird a short-tailed look, striking from below – which is often the way it is seen, as it tends to sing and feed in the canopy.

Juvenile plumage (above) is duller than the **adult's** (left), but still cleaner looking and with more contrast than in Willow Warbler or Chiffchaff.

The three common wood-loving warblers are Wood, Willow and Chiffchaff. All are olive above and pale below, but Wood Warbler is the most distinctive, greener than the other two.

GRASSHOPPER WARBLER *Locustella naevia*

13CM, 5IN

SEDGE WARBLER *Acrocephalus schoenobaenus*

13CM, 5IN

It is helpful to divide the most common warblers by their habitat preferences: waterside species, tree lovers, and scrub and bramble lovers. Often the most useful approach to identifying them is to start by narrowing them down to their most likely group. All are summer visitors only (except Dartford and Cetti's Warblers). **Grasshopper Warbler** is a small, streaky warbler that you are far more likely to hear than see – a long, high-pitched 'reeling', so called because it is not dissimilar to the sound made by an angler's reel. The bird itself spends most of its time secreted deep in thick, low vegetation, which is sometimes – but by no means always – damp. **Sedge Warbler** is a water lover, but tends to prefer the dryer edges, breeding in tangly vegetation alongside lakes, rivers and marshes over most of Britain. Fortunately, it is not a great skulker and often gives its song from a conspicuous perch, or even during its short parachuting display flight. The song is very similar to Reed Warbler's, but less repetitiously rhythmic.

Grasshopper Warbler. Often reels for a minute or more. Best heard at dawn or dusk, or even at night, but the pitch is such that some people can't hear it.

Sedge Warbler. Heavily streaked on the upperparts. Conspicuous pale stripe over the eye in adult and juvenile birds is a feature not shown by any other common British warbler. **Juvenile** (below) has a streakier pale crown than adult.

Adult Sedge Warbler (above). The streakiest of the 'waterside' warblers. Song often incorporates excitable flourishes and impersonations of other species. More varied than monotonous regular rhythm of Reed Warbler.

170

REED WARBLER *Acrocephalus scirpaceus*

12.5CM, 5IN

A good name, as Reed Warbler is very much addicted to reedbeds. It sometimes shares this habitat with Sedge Warblers, but Reed Warblers really do stay in the reeds, at least when they are breeding, for they rarely nest anywhere else. Birds on migration can occur in dryer areas, particularly on the coast, and sometimes puzzle birdwatchers. The truth is that there are a number of rare warblers that are difficult to identify, but they aren't in this book and, frankly, you are unlikely to see them unless they have already been located by other birders. Basically, Reed is a similar shape and size to Sedge Warbler, but with smooth, plain unstreaked upperparts and no obvious eyestripe (there is a very faint one). The song has a similar scratchy quality to Sedge Warbler's (hardly a warble), but it is less imaginative and excitable, with each phrase repeated rather monotonously in regular rhythm. Reed Warblers are scarce in Scotland and the Northern Isles. They are one of the most common host species of the Cuckoo.

Song is rather scratchy and monotonous, similar to the Sedge Warbler's, but less imaginative and excitable.

Upperparts a uniform warm brown. Reed warblers seldom fly far at their breeding site. They build a cup-shaped nest of woven grasses, which they sling between two or more reed stems.

LESSER WHITETHROAT *Sylvia curruca*

13.5CM, 5.25IN

Obviously related to Common Whitethroat, but actually quite easy to identify. Lesser has a duller brown back and wings, a darker mask over the cheeks, gleaming white underparts and black legs (Common's underparts are always slightly buff washed, and the legs are pinky yellow). As the name implies, Lesser is also a little smaller and less scruffy. The song starts similarly to Common's, but is shorter and often ends with a short 'rattle' (though the repeated note is quite melodious). The call is a hard 'tac' (similar to Blackcap's). Lesser Whitethroats seem to have a definite preference for mature hedgerows and are often seen a little higher from the ground than Common Whitethroats. Male builds the nest in hedgerow, leaving the female to line it. Tends to be rather more skulking than Common Whitethroat in its habits. Has white outer tail feathers, as has Common Whitethroat. Like all warblers, Lesser Whitethroats can also turn up on migration in much less typical and less vegetated habitats.

Juvenile. Paler than adult. Like other migrants, Lesser Whitethroats will put on weight by eating a lot before undertaking their long flight. Blackberries ripen at just the right time of year.

Flight is very similar to Whitethroat's, but Lesser is more skulking in its habits.

Adult. The silky white underparts are often the most conspicuous feature as it slips through vegetation.

COMMON WHITETHROAT *Sylvia communis*

14CM, 5.5IN

The most common and widespread of the scrub-loving warblers (known by birdwatchers as Sylvias because this is the first part of their scientific name). They breed in brambles, nettle beds, gorse and similar vegetation. Most conspicuous in the breeding season, when the male gives his scratchy little song, either from a perch or during his parachuting display flight. At other times Common Whitethroats can be very skulky. The male has the greyest head and the most obvious white throat, which is sometimes fluffed out, giving the bird a slightly scruffy look. Females and juveniles are duller, though the young birds do have a rather nice tawny tinge to their upperparts. Lesser Whitethroat may share not dissimilar habitats, but is duller brown on the back, and has a dark mask and black legs. Common has pinky yellow legs. It has white outer tail feathers, as has Lesser Whitethroat. The most frequently heard call is a soft, scolding 'churr'. Although like other warblers the birds are largely insectivorous, berries are an important part of their diet in autumn.

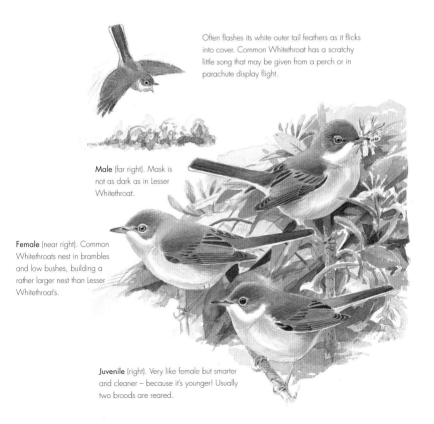

Often flashes its white outer tail feathers as it flicks into cover. Common Whitethroat has a scratchy little song that may be given from a perch or in parachute display flight.

Male (far right). Mask is not as dark as in Lesser Whitethroat.

Female (near right). Common Whitethroats nest in brambles and low bushes, building a rather larger nest than Lesser Whitethroat's.

Juvenile (right). Very like female but smarter and cleaner – because it's younger! Usually two broods are reared.

GARDEN WARBLER *Sylvia borin*

14CM, 5.5IN

Not really a very appropriate name as this species isn't often seen in gardens, unless they have been left to get thoroughly overgrown. Garden Warblers prefer the tangly, brambly edges of woodlands. They are scrub lovers, but seem to need mature trees nearby. They are clearly related to Blackcap, and – like that species – are rather slow and cumbersome movers through foliage: lumbering, rather than flitting like the more agile warblers. Most of the time they stay under cover. The plumage is very plain: a soft greyish-brown with no obvious markings, though there might be a very slight olive tinge on the neck. Garden Warbler is rather like a Blackcap without a cap. The song is very similar indeed to the Blackcap's, and often confuses even experienced ears. It contains much the same notes but is a little more compressed and less rambly, but individuals vary. Perhaps the most likely confusion species would be a dull Chiffchaff (see page 176) but note Garden Warbler's larger size and less agile movements.

Adult (below). Rarely seen out in the open, adults stay under thick cover most of the time. The species favours broadleaved or mixed woodland with dense, brambly undergrowth for nesting.

Juvenile (above). Very like the adults. A single brood is generally reared and young birds remain with the female for several weeks after leaving the nest.

BLACKCAP *Sylvia atricapilla*

14CM, 5.5IN

Similar size and jizz to Garden Warbler. Plumage is a rather leaden greyish. The male has a black cap, while the female and youngsters have chestnut-brown caps. The song is a rich warbling not unlike that of a small, speeded-up Blackbird. It sounds very like a Garden Warbler's song, but is generally more varied and less rhythmic. The call is a hard 'tac', very like a Lesser Whitethroat's. Although most of Britain's Blackcaps are summer visitors, increasing numbers are beginning to winter, often in gardens. They feed on elder, ivy and blackberries in autumn – it is thought that most of these birds are in fact continental rather than British breeders. Blackcaps become scarcer in the north and west, but otherwise breed in woods, often singing from high in the trees, but descending to brambles and undergrowth to actually build their nests. They tend to nest rather higher than Garden Warblers, and are rarely seen on the ground.

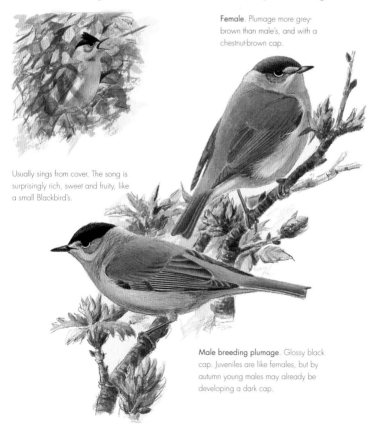

Female. Plumage more grey-brown than male's, and with a chestnut-brown cap.

Usually sings from cover. The song is surprisingly rich, sweet and fruity, like a small Blackbird's.

Male breeding plumage. Glossy black cap. Juveniles are like females, but by autumn young males may already be developing a dark cap.

CHIFFCHAFF *Phylloscopus collybita*

11CM, 4.25IN

Very similar plumage to Willow Warbler's, but fortunately its song gives its name away: 'chiff chaff, chiff chaff'. Most frequent non-breeding call is 'hooeet', similar to Willow Warbler's, though a little more monosyllabic. Increasingly in recent years, autumn birds have been heard giving a loud 'tsee u' call (the second note lower). Plumage is generally duller – browner or greyer – than Willow Warbler's, and juveniles are buff rather than yellow, but there is much variation. The legs are darker than Willow Warbler's, sometimes blackish. It is a fair rule to say that a black-legged bird must be a Chiffchaff, but a brown-legged bird could be either. The habitats of the two species overlap, but Chiffchaffs occur in coniferous woods that seem less liked by Willow Warblers. Both species nest on the ground. Continental migrants occur especially in late autumn; they are clearly of more eastern origin, and often look very grey and white. There is much variation among Chiffchaffs in Europe and Asia, and individuals often puzzle even expert birders.

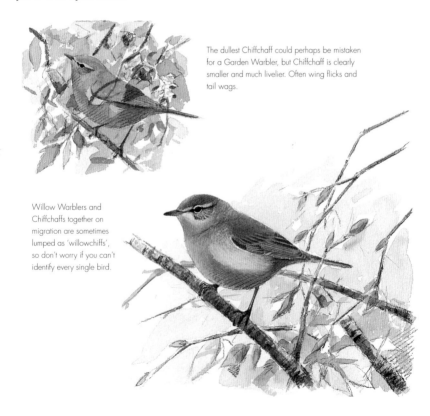

The dullest Chiffchaff could perhaps be mistaken for a Garden Warbler, but Chiffchaff is clearly smaller and much livelier. Often wing flicks and tail wags.

Willow Warblers and Chiffchaffs together on migration are sometimes lumped as 'willowchiffs', so don't worry if you can't identify every single bird.

WILLOW WARBLER *Phylloscopus trochilus*

11CM, 4.25IN

The most common and widespread British summer visitor, nesting in most parts of Britain in a variety of habitats, including areas that have few trees (let alone willows). Notoriously similar in plumage to Chiffchaff, it can only be separated with certainty by measuring the primary feathers. Brown legs usually indicate a Willow Warbler, as Chiffchaffs generally have blackish legs, but you have to be really close to the birds to see the legs. Birdwatchers sometimes refer to migrants of both species as 'willowchiffs'. Fortunately, their songs are completely different. Willow Warbler has a lovely, wispy cascading phrase, going down the scale, whilst Chiffchaff sings its name. However, both species have a similar non-breeding call: a soft 'hoo eet'. Willow Warbler's rises more on the second note, but it takes a practised ear to separate them. Willow Warbler's plumage tends to be less brown (or grey) than Chiffchaff's, but it is variable. Young birds can look very yellow on the underparts. (See also Wood Warbler, page 169.)

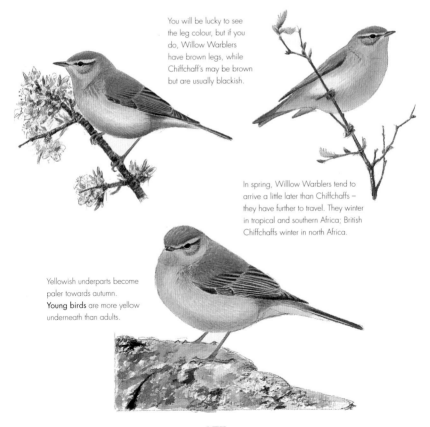

You will be lucky to see the leg colour, but if you do, Willow Warblers have brown legs, while Chiffchaff's may be brown but are usually blackish.

In spring, Willow Warblers tend to arrive a little later than Chiffchaffs – they have further to travel. They winter in tropical and southern Africa; British Chiffchaffs winter in north Africa.

Yellowish underparts become paler towards autumn.
Young birds are more yellow underneath than adults.

WAXWING *Bombycilla garrulus*

18CM, 7IN

A winter visitor from the far north of Europe and Russia, which sometimes invades Britain in large numbers, while in other years there are almost none. These irruptions depend on food supply (or rather, lack of it). Waxwings are completely addicted to red berries, so if there is a Waxwing winter, look for them on any red berry-bearing bushes and trees. The largest flocks often occur alongside supermarkets and petrol stations, where the borders have been 'decoratively' planted. Waxwings are normally very tame and allow close approach in busy areas. They may also visit gardens. They arrive – usually in October or November – mainly on the east and north-east coasts, but then move inland, sometimes reaching Ireland. They are slightly smaller than Starlings, but the pinkish-brown plumage, crest and waxy red-and-yellow-tipped wings are unique. A flock in flight, however, could easily be dismissed as Starlings, as they have a similar shape. The call is a soft sibilant trilling.

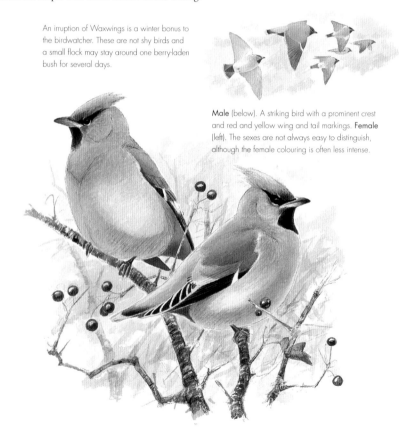

An irruption of Waxwings is a winter bonus to the birdwatcher. These are not shy birds and a small flock may stay around one berry-laden bush for several days.

Male (below). A striking bird with a prominent crest and red and yellow wing and tail markings. **Female** (left). The sexes are not always easy to distinguish, although the female colouring is often less intense.

178

TREECREEPER *Certhia familiaris*

12.5CM, 5IN

Resident in woods throughout Britain and really quite numerous, but sometimes frustratingly hard to see. It entirely lives up to its name, by creeping, almost like a hesitant little mouse, up tree trunks and along branches. It generally works its way up, then flits to the bottom of another trunk and starts to spiral upwards again. The streaky brown upperparts provide beautiful camouflage against the brown bark. In fact, it is the gleaming white underparts that are most likely to catch your eye. The call is a thin 'seeee seeee', so high-pitched that some people simply can't hear it. The song is similarly thin, but actually quite catchy: a repeated 'see see', accelerating and ending with a little flourish, 'sissi see'. Treecreepers nest in cavities in tree trunks, or behind loose bark. They often tag along with roving flocks of tits outside the breeding season.

Flies from the top of one tree to the base of another to start on the upwards climb again.

Usually nests behind a flap of bark or crevice in a tree trunk. Also roosts in cavity in soft bark.

Uses its thin, tweezer-like bill to prise under bark and probe into it for insects. Unlike Nuthatch, does not climb *down* trunks. Tail feathers strengthened like a woodpecker's.

179

NUTHATCH *Sitta europaea*

14CM, 5.5IN

Resident in mature woodland in England and Wales, but scarce in Scotland and absent from Ireland. Looks and behaves like a colourful little woodpecker, but in fact belongs to its very own family. Climbs up and down tree trunks and along branches. Can be hard to spot, but does sometimes visit garden feeders and is charmingly conspicuous. Nests in holes in trees, customizing them by plastering the openings with mud, which sets like concrete. The bird's presence in woodland is often betrayed by its calls, which include loud 'kwiks' and thin 'sees'. Its song is a ringing, repeated 'peepeepeepee' (similar to Lesser Spotted Woodpecker and Kestrel's, but not quite as hard-edged as either). The only other small bird that has similar plumage is male Wheatear (see page 198), but Wheatears have totally different habits, since they much prefer open ground and certainly don't climb trees. Nuthatches also latch onto roving tit flocks.

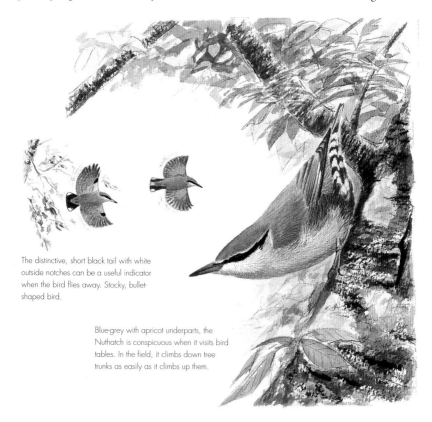

The distinctive, short black tail with white outside notches can be a useful indicator when the bird flies away. Stocky, bullet-shaped bird.

Blue-grey with apricot underparts, the Nuthatch is conspicuous when it visits bird tables. In the field, it climbs down tree trunks as easily as it climbs up them.

WREN *Troglodytes troglodytes*

9.5CM, 3.75IN

Arguably Britain's most common and widespread bird, but not perhaps obviously so, since it is small and often secretive. Wrens breed all over Britain and may be found nesting among rocks on remote islands, as well as in dense undergrowth in the corners of urban gardens. The nest is a lovely compact ball of dead leaves and moss. The bird itself is pretty unmistakable: tiny, plump and with an invariably cocked tail. It also has an extremely loud song, always incorporating a fast trill, and often delivered from a conspicuous perch, with a puffed-out breast and trembling wings. The call is a hard 'tchick tchick', and is sometimes the only hint of the bird's presence when it is in skulking mode. This habit of giving only brief glimpses has led many a birdwatcher to momentarily mistake Wrens for skulky rare warblers.

The nest is often stuffed into the tiniest crevice. Males may build several nests for a female to choose from. The female adds the lining. Males may be polygamous.

Fast and direct flight on whirring wings, though usually only for short distances.

Wrens often sing from conspicuous perches, but even if you can't see them, they make their presence felt. Always a good rule if you are in pursuit of a possible skulky rarity: ask yourself whether you are sure it isn't just a wayward Wren.

STARLING *Sturnus vulgaris*

21.5CM, 8.5IN

Breeds all over Britain, in holes in trees or crevices in rocks, cliffs and buildings. Large numbers arrive from the Continent in autumn and spend the winter in Britain. Forms large roosts, sometimes involving many thousands of birds that fly in spectacular clouds as they come in at dusk or leave at dawn. These roosts may be in trees, reedbeds or the centres of towns and cities. The Starling population in the UK – as well as on the Continent – has declined rapidly in recent years, and the species is now considered endangered. Adult Starlings may look black, but in fact their plumage is iridescent, with all colours of the rainbow, and there is extensive whitish spotting on the body feathers. Starling's song is full of scratchy whistles and trills, and often incorporates the calls of other birds, which may include Curlews and redshanks, so accurate that they even sometimes fool birdwatchers! Starlings may also impersonate human 'wolf whistles', or even phone or door bells. A migrating flock of Starlings looks rather similar to a party of Redwings (page 185), but note the triangular, pointed wing shape of Starlings.

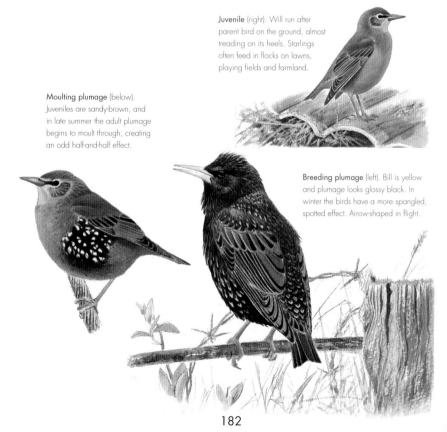

Juvenile (right). Will run after parent bird on the ground, almost treading on its heels. Starlings often feed in flocks on lawns, playing fields and farmland.

Moulting plumage (below). Juveniles are sandy-brown, and in late summer the adult plumage begins to moult through, creating an odd half-and-half effect.

Breeding plumage (left). Bill is yellow and plumage looks glossy black. In winter the birds have a more spangled, spotted effect. Arrow-shaped in flight.

DIPPER *Cinclus cinclus*

18CM, 7IN

A small, plump bird, with the looks of a thrush and the habits of a submarine! Found exclusively near fast-flowing streams, mainly in upland areas, though may descend lower during the winter, but always near water. If seen well, it is unmistakable, looking mainly black above, with a chestnut belly and a gleaming white bib. Your best chance of a good view is to wait at a bridge and scan the rocks and river banks, where the birds bob up and down before leaping into the water, often submerging in their quest for food. Grey Wagtails often share this habitat. Dippers bob and curtsey with a downwards jerk of the tail and a blink of their eyes. If close enough you may see the white eyelid. Once seen, never forgotten, but Dippers also have a habit of disappearing around the next corner without giving a decent view. The flight is very fast, low and direct. The call is a short 'zit', the song a pleasantly sweet warble. Dippers are usually solitary or in pairs, preferring the same stretch of water all year. Bridges, overhanging banks, tree roots and waterfalls provide nest sites.

Juvenile plumage. Young birds have scaly, slate-grey plumage.

Adult plumage. Mainly black above with a chestnut belly and white bib. Among songbirds the elusive Dipper is unique, diving into the water and walking or flying along the bottom searching for food. It is a strong swimmer without webbed feet.

FIELDFARE *Turdus pilaris*

25.5CM, 10IN

The larger of the winter thrushes. Arrives with Scandinavian Redwings in October and is usually gone by the end of April. A very few breed each year in northern areas. Considerably larger than Redwing – nearly as big as a Mistle Thrush – but with very distinctive and handsome plumage. Its speckly breast is on a background of yellowy buff, and no other thrush has its chestnut-brown upperparts and grey head and rump. The grey rump is particularly obvious when birds are in flight, as is the silvery leading edge to the underwing. Fieldfares are noisy birds in flight, usually making loud, excitable chacking and wheezing noises. They do travel and call at night along with Redwings, but not quite in such numbers. They feed on berries in hedgerows and nearby fields. They are almost always in flocks: indeed, it's true to say that if you see a couple of Fieldfares in a tree, there's probably a dozen. When they fly, you will often be surprised at how many were in there.

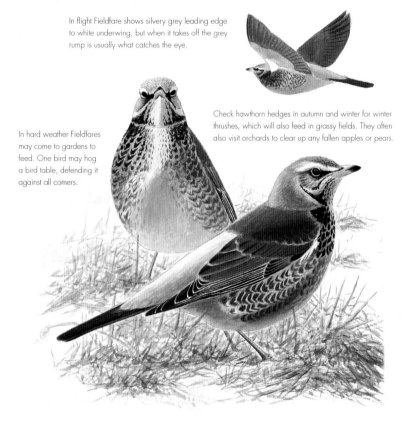

In flight Fieldfare shows silvery grey leading edge to white underwing, but when it takes off the grey rump is usually what catches the eye.

Check hawthorn hedges in autumn and winter for winter thrushes, which will also feed in grassy fields. They often also visit orchards to clear up any fallen apples or pears.

In hard weather Fieldfares may come to gardens to feed. One bird may hog a bird table, defending it against all comers.

REDWING *Turdus iliacus*

21CM, 8.25IN.

There are two species of 'winter thrush' in Britain: Redwing and Fieldfare. Both arrive in October – often in their thousands – and depart by April. A very few pairs of Redwing breed each year in Scotland or the Northern Isles. They migrate at night, and their thin, squeaky calls are often mistaken for those of bats (generally people can't actually hear bats!). Redwing is about the size of a Song Thrush, and not dissimilar in plumage, but easily identified by the vivid white stripe over the eye and white moustache. The red part of the wing is in the 'armpit', and is clearly a deeper orange than a Song Thrush's. A small red area is usually visible on the flanks of a feeding bird. Redwings are often in flocks with other thrushes, especially Fieldfares. They feed on berries – particularly those of hawthorns – and on worms, in areas of short grass. Part of our wintering population comes from Greenland and Iceland, and the rest from Scandinavia.

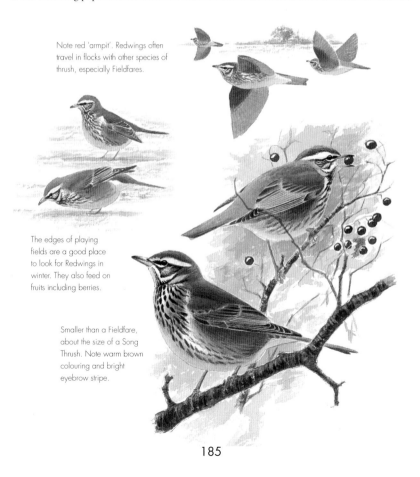

Note red 'armpit'. Redwings often travel in flocks with other species of thrush, especially Fieldfares.

The edges of playing fields are a good place to look for Redwings in winter. They also feed on fruits including berries.

Smaller than a Fieldfare, about the size of a Song Thrush. Note warm brown colouring and bright eyebrow stripe.

SONG THRUSH *Turdus philomelos*

23CM, 9IN

A resident breeding bird all over Britain wherever there are bushes or trees, and numbers are also swelled by continental immigrants in winter. Song and Mistle Thrushes are the two resident thrush species, and the most frequently confused. Song Thrush is smaller, rather less densely speckled on the underparts, with smaller spots, and lacks the rather patchy face pattern of Mistle Thrush (see opposite for other differences). In flight, Mistle Thrush shows white outer tail tips and a whitish underwing (as opposed to the cinnamon of Song Thrush). Song Thrush's song is similar to a Blackbird's, but it repeats each phrase, sometimes several times. It sometimes sings at night and gets wrongly reported as a Nightingale. In flight, it often gives a short 'tsip' call. Sadly, Song Thrushes seem to be declining as garden and farmland birds, possibly as a result of ultra-efficient snail control by pesticides. They break snails' shells on a stone 'anvil', which is left surrounded by bits of shell.

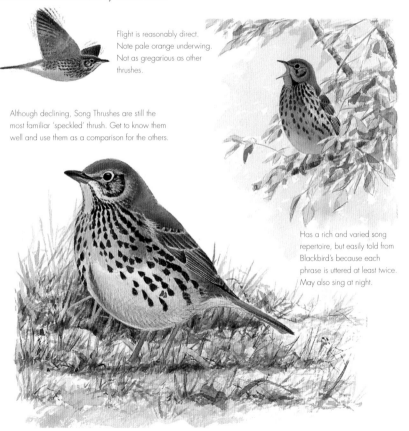

Flight is reasonably direct. Note pale orange underwing. Not as gregarious as other thrushes.

Although declining, Song Thrushes are still the most familiar 'speckled' thrush. Get to know them well and use them as a comparison for the others.

Has a rich and varied song repertoire, but easily told from Blackbird's because each phrase is uttered at least twice. May also sing at night.

MISTLE THRUSH *Turdus viscivorus*

27CM, 10.5IN

The Mistle Thrush is Britain's largest thrush, with bold, conspicuous breast spots and a grey back. It generally has less warm coloration than Song Thrush. It shows white outer tail feathers and white underwing in flight, which is characterized by the wings being closed at regular intervals, but not markedly undulating. Fieldfare has a similar flight pattern and also has a white underwing, but the upperparts are completely different. The Mistle Thrush is also called Stormcock because of its habit of singing loudly from exposed perches in bad weather. Its song is not repetitive like the Song Thrush's, nor as mellow as the Blackbird's. Call is a harsh 'churr' or rattle. Quite shy during the breeding season, but defends its territory fiercely against other bird species and even preys on the nestlings of small birds, although most of the time it relies on fruits such as berries (including those of mistletoe, of course), insects and other invertebrates. In late summer family parties often move out into more open ground. Present throughout the year, with winter migrants visiting from the Continent.

Singing loudly, if not as musically as a Blackbird or Song Thrush, from the top of an exposed perch is typical.

In flight, the white underwing soon separates Mistle from other thrushes except Fieldfare. For that, a back view is easier.

Upright stance, bold attitude and 'bouncy' gait. Mistle Thrushes do eat small snails, but a thrush bashing a snail on a stone is almost certainly a Song Thrush.

BLACKBIRD *Turdus merula*

25CM, 10IN

One of Britain's best-loved and most-familiar birds. Belongs to the thrush family. Only the male is black. Female and young Blackbirds are brown, and the juveniles can look quite orange-tinged and speckly on the breast, which gives them a more thrush-like look (compare Song and Mistle Thrushes, pages 186–7), but they never have the black breast spots or sandy upperparts of true thrushes. Blackbirds are found all over Britain, even in fairly wild and almost treeless terrain, but they are missing from the really mountainous areas. Numbers are much increased in winter by continental immigrants. The song is very rich and sometimes heard at night, giving rise to reports of Nightingales (see page 193). The 'chink chink' alarm call is also a familiar sound, and it also has a thin anxiety call, 'seeee'. Ring Ouzel is the most similar species. Particularly beware semi-albino Blackbirds that may have white on their breasts. Ring Ouzel's breast crescent is always more symmetrical (even in the duller females).

Juvenile (left). Speckled and rusty-brown. Can look very thrush-like.

Female (far right). Less warm brown than juvenile. Blackbirds take a wide variety of food – a tell-tale sign is a rhythmic rustling as they turn over leaves in the undergrowth.

Male breeding plumage (right). Vivid yellow beak. Cocks tail on landing, lowering it slowly and gracefully. A superb songster, it's a noisy bird, persistently 'chinking' at dusk.

RING OUZEL *Turdus torquatus*

24CM, 9.5IN

A summer visitor very much the high-altitude version of the Blackbird. Similar size. The male is largely black, and the females and young birds browner, though with a greyer caste than female or young Blackbirds. Male has a conspicuous white crescent on the breast, which is fainter in female and young birds. One of the best features is the silvery caste to the wings, which is particularly noticeable when the bird flies. It also frequently gives its characteristic, dry, excitable 'tac' call, which is quite unlike a Blackbird's call. Ring Ouzels generally prefer to feed on open, grassy areas, but readily escape into the cover of nearby trees, gorse or brambles. They do not, however, take to thick woodlands, as Blackbirds often do. The song is like a rather wild, simplified version of a Blackbird's song, and echoes through the valleys and slopes of its wild breeding habitat.

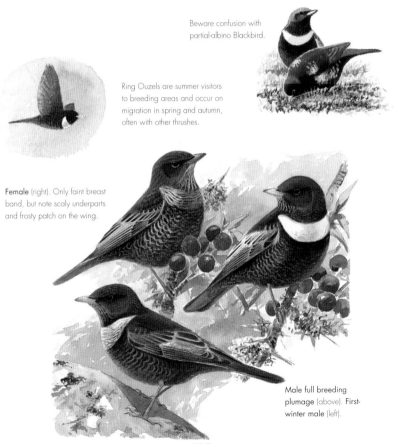

Beware confusion with partial-albino Blackbird.

Ring Ouzels are summer visitors to breeding areas and occur on migration in spring and autumn, often with other thrushes.

Female (right). Only faint breast band, but note scaly underparts and frosty patch on the wing.

Male full breeding plumage (above). First-winter male (left).

SPOTTED FLYCATCHER *Muscicapa striata*

14CM, 5.5IN

Summer visitor to Britain; rarely arrives before mid-May or even early June. Breeds throughout Britain, often nesting in foliage against a tree or wall – ivy is a favourite. Also uses open nest boxes. When catching flies, it repeatedly flits off, does an acrobatic snatch, then returns to the same or a nearby perch. Its stance is very upright. Occurs on migration at coastal locations away from trees, where it uses a rock or fence as a regular perch. Plumage is very drab: merely soft grey-brown with a few streaks on the breast and crown. Although the flycatching habits often attract your attention, remember that other species can also behave in a slightly similar manner. It is the upright pose and the constant returning to the same perch that tends to be the give-away. Female Pied Flycatcher has the same habits, but is smaller, has no streaking, and shows white on the wing bar and outer tail (see opposite). Call is a soft, high-pitched 'zeee'. Robins have a similar call.

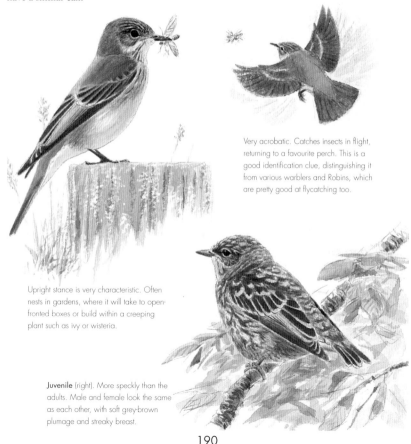

Very acrobatic. Catches insects in flight, returning to a favourite perch. This is a good identification clue, distinguishing it from various warblers and Robins, which are pretty good at flycatching too.

Upright stance is very characteristic. Often nests in gardens, where it will take to open-fronted boxes or build within a creeping plant such as ivy or wisteria.

Juvenile (right). More speckly than the adults. Male and female look the same as each other, with soft grey-brown plumage and streaky breast.

PIED FLYCATCHER *Ficedula hypoleuca*

13CM, 5IN

Summer visitor to Britain, breeding in deciduous woods – especially oak – in Wales, north-west England, some parts of Scotland and very occasionally elsewhere. Nests in holes in trees, and readily uses nest boxes. Also seen on migration at coastal locations, away from trees. Slightly smaller and neater than Spotted Flycatcher. Males in breeding plumage are unmistakably black and white. Female and juveniles (and autumn males) are dark brown above and whitish below. They have no streaking, but show a white wing bar and white outer tail feathers. These are conspicuous when the bird flies. Otherwise, they can be hard to spot, as they hide under the canopy before flitting out briefly to snatch a fly. They tend to be less addicted to favourite perches than Spotted Flycatchers. Female Chaffinch (see page 210) is also brown with white wing bars and can be reminiscent of a Pied Flycatcher. Various calls mainly with a slightly metallic quality, including a sharp ticking. The song involves two repeated notes, 'zee it, zee it', with an occasional short trill.

Can be difficult to see, flitting out briefly from the canopy. Less reliant on favourite perches than Spotted Flycatcher.

Female and juvenile (above). Dark brown with whitish underparts, but if you see one in autumn, bear in mind that the males have moulted to become dark brown too.

Male breeding plumage (left). Pied Flycatchers will breed in nest boxes (those with holes rather than the open-fronted kind), but often face competition for nest sites from Great Tits.

ROBIN *Erithacus rubecula*

14CM, 5.5IN

Possibly the best-loved and best-known bird in Britain. The adult hardly needs a description. Juveniles, however, can be puzzling, as they are speckled all over. British Robins are tame and conspicuous, but continental birds are very skulky, and when they occur in Britain on migration (which they do in considerable numbers) they are likely to keep hidden or give only brief glimpses. This behaviour has led many a birdwatcher to mistake a briefly seen Robin for any number of possible rare little brown birds. They can skulk like warblers or flit like flycatchers. If you are wondering if you are chasing a rarity, it is never a bad rule to ask yourself if it might just be a shy Robin! Fortunately, the Robin's most frequent call is very distinctive: a loud 'tick tick'. The song is full of lovely relaxed, wispy phrases; the winter version is audibly 'sadder'. Robins often sing at night, and can be mistaken for Nightingales (see opposite).

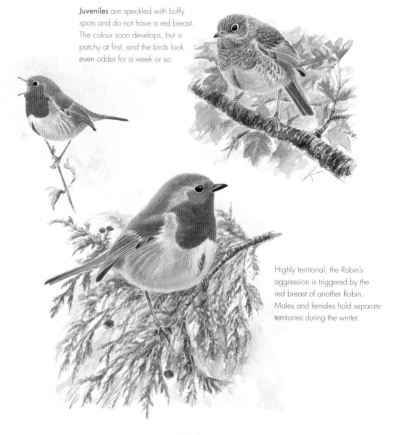

Juveniles are speckled with buffy spots and do not have a red breast. The colour soon develops, but is patchy at first, and the birds look even odder for a week or so.

Highly territorial, the Robin's aggression is triggered by the red breast of another Robin. Males and females hold separate territories during the winter.

192

NIGHTINGALE *Luscinia megarhynchos*

16.5CM, 6.5IN

Nightingales are summer visitors and occur in only relatively few areas of south-eastern England. If you hear a bird singing at night, at any time except spring and early summer, or away from the south and east, it is *not* a Nightingale. The confusions arise because several species often sing at night: particularly Robin, Song Thrush and Blackbird. Nightingales like open woodland with dense thickets, often near heathland. They don't occur in town (so the bird that sang in Berkeley Square wasn't one!). Nightingale's song is indeed very rich and fruity, incorporating various trills and drawn-out whistles, and is delivered just as much during the day as at night. Nightingales are a little bigger and more slender than a Robin, warm brown above, paler below, and with a distinct rufous tinge to the tail. Not dissimilar to a female Common Redstart, but this is smaller, and the red tail contrasts more with the rest of the plumage and is 'trembled' frequently (see page 195).

Juvenile. Spotted and looks rather like a big young Robin.

Adult. Warm brown above, pale below. Nightingales are real skulkers and you rarely get a good view of one. When you do, you realize it isn't much to look at!

BLACK REDSTART *Pheonicurus ochruros*

14CM, 5.5IN

The same size and jizz as a Common Redstart, but the male is very dark grey, and actually black on the face and breast, with white flashes in the wing, whilst the female is merely dingy all over. Both species have the typical quivering orangey tail. Black Redstarts, however, do not occur in woods. They prefer rocks or even concrete, and in fact their favourite breeding places are ruined buildings, power stations and factories, mainly in central and south-eastern England. At such places they sing from rooftop perches. The song is an accelerating warble (a little like a Chaffinch's) ending in a rattly trill. The call is a hard 'tuck'. Black Redstarts stay in Britain in winter and usually move down to the coasts, where they may frequent shingly beaches or rocky shorelines. There is also a noticeable passage, especially in October, when they often favour newly ploughed fields (as do other migrants, such as Wheatears). Any redstart in winter will thus be a Black. However, Black is never as numerous a migrant as Common can be.

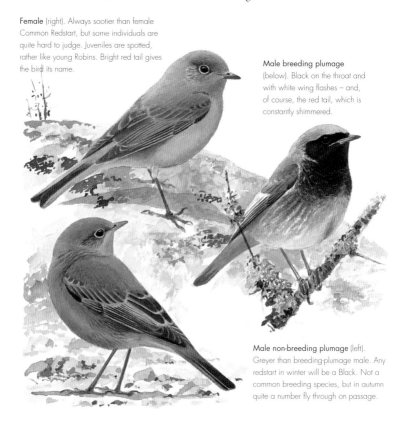

Female (right). Always sootier than female Common Redstart, but some individuals are quite hard to judge. Juveniles are spotted, rather like young Robins. Bright red tail gives the bird its name.

Male breeding plumage (below). Black on the throat and with white wing flashes – and, of course, the red tail, which is constantly shimmered.

Male non-breeding plumage (left). Greyer than breeding-plumage male. Any redstart in winter will be a Black. Not a common breeding species, but in autumn quite a number fly through on passage.

COMMON REDSTART *Phoenicurus phoenicurus*

14CM, 5.5IN

A summer visitor, quite widely distributed in Britain but by no means common. Breeds in woods, parkland and the edges of heaths or moorland, but requires mature trees with nesting holes. About the size of a Robin, but slimmer and with the tail invariably held down. The male in breeding plumage is very striking, with a black bib, deep orange-red breast, and orange rump and tail. Female is much duller: generally fawn, with only the tail orange. Young males can show partial breeding plumage. Redstarts habitually quiver or tremble their tails. The call is a loud 'hoo eet'. (Unfortunately, several other species also give 'hooeet' calls, for example Chaffinch, Willow Warbler and Chiffchaff.) This call is often incorporated into the jangling little song. Common Redstarts also occur on migration at coastal sites, which may be completely treeless. At such times and places, Black Redstarts may also occur. Both male and female Black Redstart are uniformly dark, except for the tail, but the palest females are only a few shades duskier than a female Common Redstart.

Male breeding plumage (below). Starts to look more like female (though still darker) by autumn migration.

Female (right). Duller than male with only tail orange. Common Redstart nests in mature trees such as oak, with suitable holes, though it occasionally also uses walls or nests on the ground.

Young male (left). Just a hint of the black throat coming into view.

WHINCHAT *Saxicola rubetra*

12.5CM, 5IN

Slightly smaller and slimmer than a Robin. A summer visitor breeding in open heathland and young conifer plantations, especially in the north and west of Britain. Also turns up on migration, sometimes in less rural areas such as playing fields and allotments. Whinchats make themselves conspicuous by perching on the tops of bushes, dead plants, fences and even telegraph wires. Most similar in plumage and habits to Stonechat, but Stonechats are dumpier and lack the obvious white eyebrow stripe and 'capped' appearance of Whinchat. Whinchat also has white sides to the base of the tail, most noticeable in males when they fly or land. At a distance Whinchat can be mistaken for a Wheatear, which is a similar shape and also often perches in similar habitats, but note Wheatear's vivid white rump as soon as it flies. Males are brighter than females and juveniles, with blacker ears and upperparts. Song is similar to Stonechat's and call is 'tic-tic', but it is almost always silent away from the breeding areas.

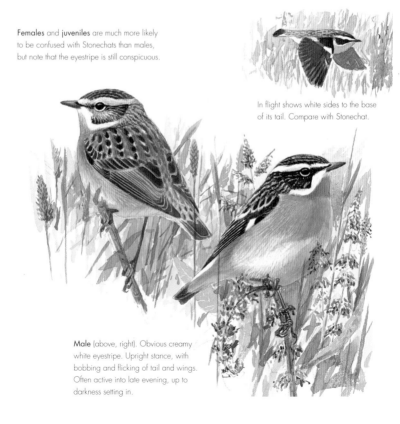

Females and **juveniles** are much more likely to be confused with Stonechats than males, but note that the eyestripe is still conspicuous.

In flight shows white sides to the base of its tail. Compare with Stonechat.

Male (above, right). Obvious creamy white eyestripe. Upright stance, with bobbing and flicking of tail and wings. Often active into late evening, up to darkness setting in.

STONECHAT *Saxicola torquata*

12.5CM, 5IN

A dumpy little bird – slightly smaller than a Robin, but rather similar in shape – that makes itself conspicuous by perching on bushes, dead plants, fences and telegraph wires. Breeds on moors and heathland, especially where there is gorse. In winter moves to lower areas, including waste ground and saltmarshes. Numbers are swelled by continental migrants in late autumn. Most easily confused with Whinchat, which has similar habits. Look at the head: Stonechat does not have a whitish eyestripe, and in flight it lacks the Whinchat's white sides to the tail. Male has an obvious black head with a white half collar, and an orange breast; females and juveniles are much duller and spottier. They could be confused with young speckly Robins (page 192) or moulty Common Redstarts (page 195), but neither is likely to perch out in the open so much. Moulting Stonechats can look particularly scruffy and odd, and have been known to puzzle birdwatchers. The call is a sharp 'tsak tsak' (like clinking pebbles), which may attract your attention to the bird.

In flight shows white patch on wing, but not the white sides to tail as in Whinchat.

Female. Similar jizz and habits to Whinchat, but lacks the white eyebrow.

Juvenile. Spotty – or is it 'messy'?

Male fresh breeding plumage. Gorse is a favourite bush to perch upon and proclaim territory.

WHEATEAR *Oenanthe oenanthe*

14.5–15CM, 5.75–6IN

A summer visitor and in fact often the first migrant to arrive in spring (early March). Larger and slimmer than Robin. Prefers open habitats, often with few or no trees. Breeds on uplands, but occurs on migration both inland and on the coast, often on playing fields or mown turf (for example around reservoirs). Rather bizarrely, the male shares its lovely colour scheme with the entirely woodland-loving Nuthatch (page 180), and I have heard of the species being confused by a beginner looking at pictures in a book, but not reading the text! Wheatears don't creep up tree trunks. Wheaters do perch on bushes and walls, and even sometimes on the tops of isolated trees, and at a distance their jizz is not dissimilar to a Whinchat's. Note the lack of Whinchat's white eyestripe, and the white rump as soon as it flies. The call is a hard 'chack chack', and it has a rather squeaky wheezy song, often delivered in flight. It also sometimes hovers like a tiny Kestrel in search of food.

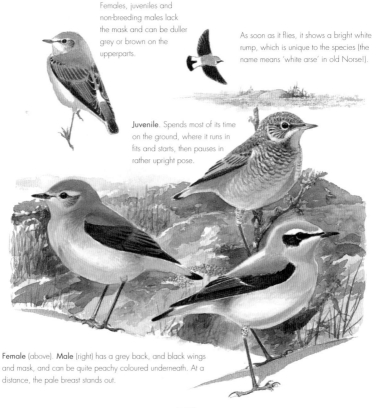

Females, juveniles and non-breeding males lack the mask and can be duller grey or brown on the upperparts.

As soon as it flies, it shows a bright white rump, which is unique to the species (the name means 'white arse' in old Norse!).

Juvenile. Spends most of its time on the ground, where it runs in fits and starts, then pauses in rather upright pose.

Female (above). **Male** (right) has a grey back, and black wings and mask, and can be quite peachy coloured underneath. At a distance, the pale breast stands out.

DUNNOCK *Prunella modularis*

14.5CM, 5.75IN

Sometimes also called Hedge Sparrow, but it is not a true sparrow (sparrows are seed-eaters with stubby bills). Actually belongs to the accentor family (yet another name is Hedge Accentor), which comprises small, fairly secretive birds with thin beaks. Dunnocks are found all over Britain, and – though they prefer foliage – they also occur in quite remote and bleak habitats. Both male and female are dingy brown on the upperparts, with strong streaking, and have a grey head and breast with a slightly bluish tinge. Although this is a rather featureless plumage, there is really nothing else like it. Female House Sparrow is most similar, but is instantly identified by its stubby beak. Dunnocks typically feed on the ground, in the shade, and they hop with little shuffly movements. They frequently flick their wings. The call is a loud 'tseep', and the song an attractive wispy but quite busy warble – a bit like a Wren's call, but without the power or the trill.

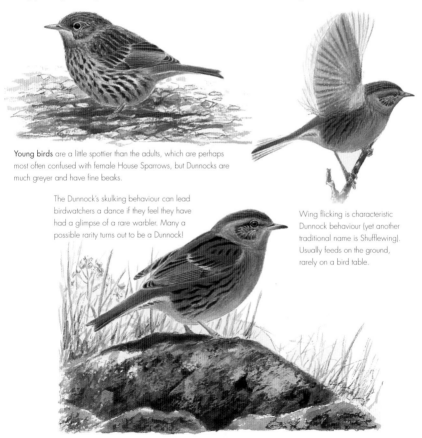

Young birds are a little spottier than the adults, which are perhaps most often confused with female House Sparrows, but Dunnocks are much greyer and have fine beaks.

The Dunnock's skulking behaviour can lead birdwatchers a dance if they feel they have had a glimpse of a rare warbler. Many a possible rarity turns out to be a Dunnock!

Wing flicking is characteristic Dunnock behaviour (yet another traditional name is Shufflewing). Usually feeds on the ground, rarely on a bird table.

HOUSE SPARROW *Passer domesticus*

14.5CM, 5.75IN

A familiar and widespread resident, usually in the vicinity of buildings of some kind, even if it's only derelict farms or ruins. The male is very distinctive, only confusable with Tree Sparrow. Note that House Sparrow has a grey centre to the crown (all brown in Tree Sparrow), larger and messier black bib, and no cheek spot. Female and juvenile House Sparrows are much duller, and with a poor view can be confused with juvenile Greenfinch (see page 212). Stray birds in odd places – for example skulking in low cover on a coastal headland – have caused birdwatchers to hope for something rarer on more than one occasion. House Sparrows nest in a variety of places, including holes in trees and buildings, and may even build an untidy nest in a hedge. They chirrup rather than sing, though they can string a number of chirrups together when they are displaying or agitated.

Male. As well as nesting under the eaves of houses, House Sparrows may also take over old House Martin nests, or build in the lower structure of larger nests.

In winter even the **male** House Sparrow (above) loses its colours, the crown and bib becoming flecked with white.

Female and **juvenile**. The archetypal little dull brown birds, lacking the male's dark bib and head markings. They can be confused with young Greenfinches.

TREE SPARROW *Passer montanus*

14CM, 5.75IN

Becoming increasingly scarce, probably due to loss of habitat caused by modern farming methods. Nevertheless, it still breeds in various parts of Britain, though it is rare in northern Scotland. Forms small flocks out of the breeding season, but these involve far fewer birds than was the case 20 or 30 years ago. A good place to look for Tree Sparrows is in farm stockyards, where they may join other seed-eaters on spilt grain. Both male and female have the same plumage, and even the juveniles are not as different as in most species. Rather like a smaller, neater version of male House Sparrow, but note that the cap is entirely chestnut-brown (not grey-centred as in House Sparrow), the bib is smaller and neater, and there is a conspicuous black cheek spot and narrow white collar. It hardly has a song, but the call is a distinctive short, sharp 'tchek'. Nests in holes in trees and buildings, and sometimes takes over old Sand Martins' nests, or uses nest boxes meant for tits.

Juvenile (right). Greyish centre to crown merging into rusty brown on sides, and with only a suggestion (or lack) of cheek spot.

Male and **female**. Similar plumage to each other. Neat black bib, cheek spot and rich chestnut cap separate them from male House Sparrows. More retiring than House Sparrows and less associated with human habitation, Tree Sparrows tend to live in open woodland, hedgerows and orchards.

YELLOW WAGTAIL *Motacilla flava*

16.5CM, 6.5IN

A summer visitor, so any wagtail with yellow on it during the winter months will be a Grey. Yellow Wagtail breeds in damp meadows and marshes, more usually (but not exclusively) near the sea or large inland waters. Mainly found in central and south-eastern England; it also occurs on passage, but is a scarce bird in Scotland and particularly in Ireland. Male is bright yellow below and olive above (unlike the grey of Grey Wagtail). Female and young birds are much duller, and some can be quite brown and washed out, but there is always a tinge of yellow. Juveniles often have a few dark flecks across the upper breast, and can slightly resemble a large pipit (particularly the rare Tawny Pipit). The call is a loud 'fsweep', which may draw attention to birds flying over. Several races of Yellow Wagtail occur in Britain on migration (and may very occasionally breed), but none is anything like as common as the basic all-yellow form. The most frequent is Blue-headed Wagtail, which does indeed have a pale blue head.

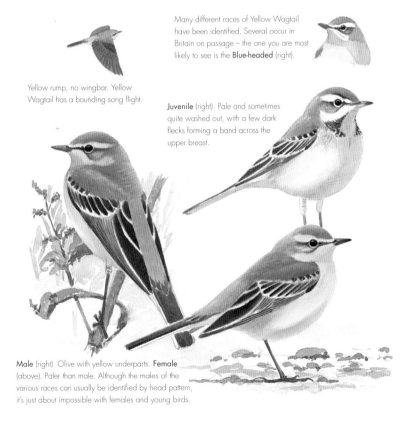

Many different races of Yellow Wagtail have been identified. Several occur in Britain on passage – the one you are most likely to see is the **Blue-headed** (right).

Yellow rump, no wingbar. Yellow Wagtail has a bounding song flight.

Juvenile (right). Pale and sometimes quite washed out, with a few dark flecks forming a band across the upper breast.

Male (right). Olive with yellow underparts. **Female** (above). Paler than male. Although the males of the various races can usually be identified by head pattern, it's just about impossible with females and young birds.

GREY WAGTAIL *Motacilla cinerea*

18CM, 7IN

Grey above but lemon yellow below, with the colour particularly strong under the tail. The male has a black bib. Breeds near fast-flowing streams, mainly in upland areas, but sometimes near – or even in – towns or villages. Your best chance of seeing them is usually from a bridge, scanning along the river banks. The birds teeter among pebbles and on stones. In winter they move to lower locations, which may include urban lakes or canals and nearby rooftops. The call is shorter than a Pied Wagtail's, with more of a 'zing' to it: a sharp 'tzit'. It may share its habitat with Pied Wagtail; but would very rarely be seen alongside Yellow Wagtail, so confusion shouldn't occur. If you can see the leg colour, Grey Wagtail's legs are pink and Yellow's are black. In flight, Grey has a longer tail that looks exceptionally narrow at the base, and this can be noticeable even at a considerable distance.

Grey sports the longest tail of all its family, narrow and black with white outer feathers. A delight to watch, perched on a boulder as this **female** is, or flying out over the water chasing insects.

Male summer plumage. Distinctive black throat. Grey is usually solitary, but a few may feed together along stretches of water where insects are plentiful.

PIED WAGTAIL *Motacilla alba*

18CM, 7IN

There are three common species of British wagtail, all well named, in that they do indeed have long tails that they wag. Otherwise, they all look very different and have differing habitat preferences. Pied Wagtail is the most numerous and widespread. Breeds all over Britain, often – but not always – near water, and forms large roosting flocks in winter, often gathering in very urban areas such as factories and car parks. Pied Wagtail nests often play host to Cuckoo. Both male and female are pied (black and white), though the female has a greyer back and smaller black bib. Young birds have a messier and slightly brown-tinged plumage. The call is best remembered as 'chiswick' (as in the London Borough of). The continental race – known as White Wagtail – occurs on passage in small numbers, particularly in spring. The flight is bounding (undulating), and the birds often call as they fly. Often seen near or among buildings and may even nest there.

The continental **White Wagtail** (right) shows very much paler grey upperparts than Pied Wagtail and is not found in large groups.

Juvenile (left). Brownish-grey in colour, and dirty white when compared with the smart pied appearance of the adult.

Male breeding plumage (right). Entirely black upperparts except for white forehead and cheeks. Black wings with prominent white edgings to all main feathers. Large black bib on otherwise white underparts. Bill, eyes and legs black in both sexes.

Female breeding plumage. Greyer back than male and less black on head and breast.

TREE PIPIT *Anthus trivialis*

15CM, 6IN

A summer visitor, so any winter pipit won't be a Tree Pipit. Breeds in open, heathy-type woodlands, often in the same sort of habitat as Woodlarks. Requires a few large trees, where it can perch right on the tops, often delivering part of its song. The full song, however, is usually given in flight. It is often this that draws attention to the bird's presence. Away from the breeding areas Tree Pipits occur as passage migrants, often in company with Meadow Pipits, and frequently in treeless areas. The call is a distinctive hoarse 'teeze'. The plumage is very similar to a Meadow Pipit's, though there are some rather subtle differences, such as slightly pinker legs, a faint yellowy wash on the breast, and a more obvious bar (greater coverts) on the closed wing. If it takes cover in a tree, it tends to creep along a branch gently wagging its tail. Note, however, that Meadow Pipits *do* sometimes perch in trees. Does not occur in flocks like Meadow Pipits.

Like most pipits, Tree Pipit is a ground-feeding and nesting bird, but it quickly flies to seek cover in a tree if disturbed.

Male Tree Pipit (above) rises from its perch and begins singing near the peak of ascent, continuing with a descending 'twsee wee wee' as it parachutes down, wings and tail spread, to land on the same perch.

Best distinguished from Meadow Pipit by its call and song flight. It also happens to have a shorter hind claw, but you won't see that.

ROCK PIPIT *Anthus petrosus*

17CM, 6.5IN

Not a bad name, as Rock Pipits do very much prefer rocky coastlines, although they also occasionally crop up on inland reservoirs (usually concrete ones) – but Meadow Pipits also occur in the same areas. A little larger than Meadow Pipit, and darker and greyer, with noticeably darker legs, often with a dark red tinge (Meadow Pipits tend to be pinky or yellowy). The outer tail feathers are smoky grey, not white. Well camouflaged among the rocks, this bird is often unseen until it takes to the wing. The call is often written as 'fist', and is similar to Meadow Pipit's, but distinguishable with experience. Found all around Britain, but scarce in south-east England. Never forms flocks as large as those of Meadow Pipit: you rarely see more than a dozen or so together, even in winter. Nests in crevices and is known to be a host species for Cuckoos. It has a typical pipit song flight, rising up from a rock on the shoreline and singing as it descends, ending with the characteristic trill.

Rock Pipit's flight song is similar to Meadow's but louder and stronger and perhaps rather more musical. Its call is fuller and more metallic.

Adults. Rock Pipit is a resident bird, usually staying within its chosen territory. It may be seen searching out insects and small molluscs among the rocks and seaweed of the shoreline.

WATER PIPIT *Anthus spinoletta*

17CM, 6.5IN

Once considered the same species as Rock Pipit, but it is clearly different and now accepted as such. A winter visitor only, to certain favoured sites, mainly sewage farms, cress beds, freshwater marshes and river foreshores. Around a hundred Water Pipits are recorded in Britain each year, most frequently in the south and east of England. The earliest sightings are usually in October, and by April most birds have returned to their breeding grounds high in the mountains of central and southern Europe. Much the same build as Rock Pipit, but brown rather than greyish upperparts, and with a whitish stripe above the eye, and white (not grey) outer tail feathers. The call is 'fist', similar to that of a Rock Pipit. The streaking on the underparts reduces as winter goes on, and by spring some birds attain breeding plumage. This is very attractive, with a bluey-grey back and almost unstreaked underparts, flushed with pink. I once saw a migrant like this on a dry coastal headland: at a distance, it looked rather like a male Wheatear (see page 198).

Pure white outer tail feathers and a pale stripe over the eye are hallmarks of Water Pipit. Very similar to Meadow Pipit in song.

Adults in the attractive pale colours of **breeding plumage** (above) and the darker **shades of winter** (right). This rare winter visitor has dark legs similar to the Rock Pipit's. At the best of times Water Pipit is difficult to observe. It tends to fly off as soon as seen and move a long distance before alighting again.

MEADOW PIPIT *Anthus pratensis*

14CM, 6IN

Pipits are small, streaky brown birds with fine, thin beaks; they spend most of their time on the ground, usually in short grass. All British species have white (or whitish) outer tail feathers; in this respect they are similar to larks. Meadow Pipit is by far the most numerous and widespread species. It is by no means confined to meadows. It may well be the only small breeding bird on remote moorland, and in winter it often occurs in all kinds of habitat, from sewage farms to saltmarshes, and even on urban wasteland. Meadow Pipit migration is in fact very complex, with some British birds going south in winter and north in spring, and other continental birds arriving in autumn. There are some days at coastal locations when the headlands seem to be alive with Meadow Pipits. They also travel inland routes. Tree Pipit is very similar in plumage, but is only a summer visitor, though it may occur in similar (treeless) areas on passage. By far the best distinction is call, and fortunately pipits invariably call when they fly.

In the breeding season Meadow Pipit displays with an attractive song flight, rising with a wispy crescendo, then parachuting down with a series of sweeter notes ending in a trill.

Out of the breeding season the species' call is a thin 'tseep', a clear sound that often attracts the attention of migrating birds overhead.

Pipits are similar to larks, but have more slender beaks and are generally slimmer and more slender-winged.

BULLFINCH *Pyrrhula pyrrhula*

14.5–16CM, 5.75–6.25IN

Occurs all over Britain and breeds in woodland with bushy edges, but never particularly numerous or conspicuous. Because of its taste for the buds of fruit trees in orchards, it is sometimes considered a pest and is accordingly persecuted: maybe that's why it's so shy. Usually seen in pairs or in small parties, rarely into double figures. The male's rich pink underparts are replaced by a soft fawn in the female, while youngsters at first lack the black cap. In flight, the most conspicuous feature is its white rump, which is often all you glimpse as it slips away into the foliage. The call is a soft, piping 'phew' that often betrays the bird's presence, challenging you to actually see it. In some autumns continental immigrants arrive on the east coast and a few stay to winter, but – unlike most other small, seed-eating birds – they never seem to join mixed flocks on stubble fields. Nests in thick hedges and dense evergreen shrubs.

Juvenile (below). Lacks the adults' black cap, but in flight the white rump and short, conical bill are good indicators.

Female (right). Bullfinches usually go around in pairs, and appear to be monogamous. It is thought that they retain the same mate in successive breeding seasons, assuming both survive.

Male (above). Looks bold in black and shocking pink, but Bullfinches are shy – not surprising considering their liking for fruit buds, though this tends to be when other seeds have failed.

209

CHAFFINCH *Fringilla coelebs*

15CM, 6IN

Perhaps surprisingly, one of the most common birds in Britain. Chaffinches are found in just about every type of habitat in all areas. Nevertheless they seem to be decreasing, possibly as a result of weed control on farmland, which reduces their food supply. They are, however, still common birds whose numbers are considerably swelled in winter by Scandinavian immigrants. Migrating flocks are often noticeable, especially in October, when they may travel alongside other finches such as Bramblings, Siskins and Linnets. Brambling is similar in shape and size, but is a winter visitor and much rarer. Chaffinch's song is a fruity warble that accelerates and ends with a flourish. The most common call is a sharp, ringing 'pink', but it also give a loud 'hooeet' (similar to both Common Redstart and Willow Warbler's calls) and other short, wheezy calls. Female Chaffinches glimpsed flitting around in treetops can momentarily resemble female Pied Flycatchers (which also have white wing bars and a white outer tail). Remember that Pied Flycatchers are only summer visitors to relatively few areas, but if you get a good view of them you will not mistake them.

Male. Very distinctive in breeding plumage, with powder-blue head, steel-blue beak and pink breast. Outside the breeding season, the beak is paler.

Double white wing bar and white outer tail feathers are conspicuous in flight. Sometimes you can see the male's greenish rump.

Male winter plumage. On the ground, Chaffinches move with a hesitant, shuffling little hop, almost as if they are limping.

Female and **young birds**. Smooth brown, with a double white wing bar – almost like a female House Sparrow, were it not for the wing bars.

BRAMBLING *Fringilla montifringilla*

14.5CM, 5.75IN

The winter version of the Chaffinch. Variable numbers arrive in October to spend the winter in Britain. In some years the species is quite widespread, but it is always scarce in Ireland. Particularly fond of beechmast and – in a good year – large flocks may form in favoured areas. Generally, though, this is a bird that you are perhaps most likely to see flying away or overhead, often in the company of Chaffinches. The most noticeable feature in flight is the white rump. Bramblings lack the white outer tail feathers of Chaffinch. The call is also very distinctive, a soft 'chuck chuck' (almost inaudible) followed by a loud, harsh 'tsweek'. I remember it as 'chuckle and squeak'! Seen on the ground, a Brambling is immediately reminiscent of a Chaffinch, but notice the orange tones on the underparts and shoulder, and the darker streaky head pattern. In fact, breeding-plumage males have black heads, but they are rarely seen in Britain except in late spring, especially in the Northern Isles before the birds return to Scandinavia.

Male. Becomes darker as spring approaches and the tips of its feathers wear away to reveal full breeding plumage, but this is unlikely to be seen in Britain.

In flight, note the oval-shaped white rump patch and white wing bar.

Female. Orangey tones on the underparts and on the shoulder; like males though not quite as bright, but with greyer heads.

GREENFINCH *Carduelis chloris*

14.5CM, 5.75IN

Common all over Britain, including in parks and gardens. Numbers are swelled by continental immigrants in autumn and winter. Male Greenfinch is very distinctive. Females and juveniles are both duller and/or streakier, and can be confused with other species. Female House Sparrow (see page 200) is browner still, with a pale eyestripe. Female and juvenile Common Crossbills (see page 215) look very similar, and Greenfinches also tend to like fir trees, where crossbills occur. Moreover, Greenfinch's single-note flight call is also rather crossbill-like. However, even the dingiest Greenfinch shows a hint of yellow along its wing and at its tail base, and it has a pale pointed bill (i.e. not crossed). Song is rather canary-like, involving a long, nasal 'dzweeee'. This is often delivered during a bat-like, fluttery song flight. The full flight call is a distinctive one note almost trilled, 'titititi', but there is also a single-note version that is less easy to be sure of.

Male (left) and **female** (below). The only other greenish finch is Siskin, but Greenfinch is clearly much bigger, with a pale bill, and is largely unstreaked. A typical seed-eater, with a large conical bill.

Note yellow flash along the outer edge of the wing – not wing bars (as in Siskin); also yellow at base of tail. Often forms flocks with House Sparrows, Chaffinches and buntings.

Young bird (left). Browner and more streaked than adults. It can sometimes be mistaken for Common Crossbill, a far less common or widespread species.

GOLDFINCH *Carduelis carduelis*

12CM, 4.75IN

A common resident in Britain, except for the far north of Scotland. The best place to look for Goldfinches is on thistle heads, which they probe with their rather long, pointy beaks. The largest flocks build up in autumn, but some of our Goldfinches then migrate further south, and a few arrive from the Continent to winter in Britain. Male and female are very distinctive, but the juveniles lack the black, white and red face markings of the adults. Broad golden wing bar is the best feature. Siskin (see page 214) is perhaps the only small finch that can look a bit similar, but note its double wing bar, streaky plumage and overall much greener tone. Goldfinch call is a tinkly twitter, which makes it easy to pick up when flying over. The song has much the same quality, but is longer and involves a few more wheezy notes and phrases.

Juvenile. Duller than adults, with streaks and lacking the distinctive face markings. Wing markings, including golden wing bar, are the best clue.

In flight, shows broad golden wing bar. Often calls, a tinkling twittering sound, like tiny bells.

The red face feathers are quite coarse, giving protection against sharp thistles and bristly teasels – favourite foods of the Goldfinch, whose thin, pointy beak is ideal for tweaking out seeds.

The sexes are similar. In autumn and winter Goldfinches often join flocks with other seed-eaters such as Greenfinches, Linnets and Sparrows.

SISKIN *Carduelis spinus*

12CM, 4.75IN

Breeds in conifer woods, especially in Scotland, Wales and Ireland. Otherwise mainly a winter visitor to southern regions. Look for Siskins particularly in alder trees, and to a lesser extent birches, usually in small flocks, but sometimes up to a hundred or more. They also feed on nut bags in gardens. In flight, the birds stay in a very close flock and have a fast, bouncy style. They almost invariably call: a soft piping 'tseu'. The twittery song is full of canary-like wheezing: like a speeded-up Greenfinch! Apart from at the breeding areas, the song is sometimes heard from wintering birds on warm spring mornings. The males have the darker crowns and bibs, and they become blackest in the breeding plumage. The dullest females and juveniles look rather like Lesser Redpolls (see opposite), which favour the same habitats and tree species but are browner. Siskins always have a tinge of yellow somewhere, especially on the wing bars.

Male (right). Becomes darker as the breeding season approaches. Often quite tame little birds, Siskins will allow a close approach. They tend to breed in conifers.

Yellow wing bars in flight not really as noticeable as those of Goldfinch and Greenfinch. Compare also female and juvenile Common Crossbill.

Commonly feeds in winter with Lesser Redpolls, on birch and alder seeds. Female (right) and juveniles can be confused with Lesser Redpolls.

Juvenile (left). Siskins are increasingly reported as garden birds, where they are attracted to bright red bags of peanuts.

LESSER REDPOLL *Carduelis caberet*

13–15CM, 5–6IN

COMMON CROSSBILL *Loxia curvirostra*

16.5CM, 6.5IN

Lesser Redpoll breeds all over Britain, mainly in young conifer plantations. It is clearly browner than Siskins – lacking any yellow tones – with white wing bars. The males have the reddest foreheads, and may have a raspberry flush in the throat as well. Different races occur, which may look frostier in general plumage, with paler rumps. Juvenile Linnet and Twite (see page 216) are similar in size and jizz to Lesser Redpolls. **Common Crossbills** breed exclusively in conifers, but are by no means present in all plantations. However, they are prone to 'irrrupting' in some years – probably due to variable pine crops – and will suddenly breed in a new area, only to desert it the following season.

Female Common Crossbill (below). Smooth dull green or almost brown; juveniles are streaked. They are not dissimilar to Greenfinches, which may occur in similar woodland and also have a short 'gip' call.

Female Lesser Redpoll (left, below) and **winter male** (above). Though the species was formerly more common than Siskin, the situation recently seems to have reversed. Flocks form in winter, especially in alders and birches.

Adult male Common Crossbill. Unmistakable, pink all over, though darker on the back. Young males are less red: almost as if they haven't fully ripened! Flight call: a liquid 'chip chip chip'.

Male (above, right) Lesser Redpoll's call is a slightly zingy 'chi chi chi', and the song adds a cheery, rattling trill to this. Both call and song are often given in flight.

LINNET *Carduelis cannabina*

13.5CM, 5.25IN

TWITE *Carduelis flavirostris*

13.5CM, 5.25IN

Linnet is resident in most parts of Britain, except north-west Scotland, where it is replaced by Twite. Particularly partial to heathy scrubby areas with gorse, but also breeds in farmland hedges and even in tangly gardens. Also occurs on migration, when continental birds may be involved. Flocks out of the breeding season often join with other seed-eaters on rough ground, stubble or saltmarshes. Linnet's flight call is a dry twittering that is surprisingly easy to get to know and recognize. The song incorporates this twitter, along with various wheezy calls and whistles. **Twite** is very much the highland version of the Linnet, but by no means present on all uplands in Britain. It has a rather limited distribution: in the Pennines, in Scotland and on the west coast of Ireland. Small numbers also winter at certain favoured locations in the south. Flight call: 'cheweet' – a little more explosive and drawn out than Linnet's. Song rather similar to Linnet's but twangier. Nests in heather, crevices in rocks and stone walls.

Female Linnet (left) and juvenile. Streaked upperparts and flanks. Best identification feature is frosty white wing flashes, a feature shown by none of the other small streaky finches.

Male Linnet (far left). Red flushes on head and breast that make it look as though it has been dipped in raspberry juice.

Male and female Twite. The sexes look the same: small, brown and streaky, with a pale yellowish bill in winter (dark in summer). Males in breeding plumage may show a slightly pink rump.

216

HAWFINCH *Coccothraustes coccothraustes*

18CM, 7IN

A large, striking finch that is nevertheless extremely difficult to see. Resident in woodlands – with a particular liking for Hornbeams and cherry orchards – mainly in England and a few parts of Wales and southern Scotland. Absent from Ireland. Your best chance of seeing one is probably if you hear its call, then catch a glimpse as it – or they – flits across the top of the canopy. The call is a sharp 'tzik' similar to a Robin's (but Robins don't often venture to the very tops of woodland trees). While searching for Hawfinches briefly glimpsed Chaffinches often lead you astray, as they too flash white wing bars, but – as is the case with so many scarce birds – the rule is that when you see it, you'll know! Hawfinches really are very handsome indeed, and well worth the patience required to see them. A few migrants occur, usually in October, and may then even appear in relatively treeless areas on the coast, but they won't stop long.

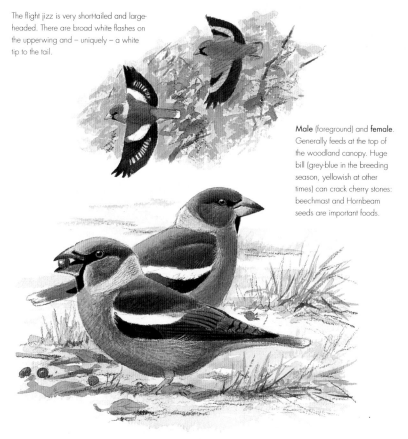

The flight jizz is very short-tailed and large-headed. There are broad white flashes on the upperwing and – uniquely – a white tip to the tail.

Male (foreground) and **female**. Generally feeds at the top of the woodland canopy. Huge bill (grey-blue in the breeding season, yellowish at other times) can crack cherry stones: beechmast and Hornbeam seeds are important foods.

SNOW BUNTING *Plectrophenax nivalis*

16.5CM, 6.5IN

A few Snow Bunting pairs breed on the almost inaccessible mountain tops of Scotland. Otherwise, this is a winter visitor from the Arctic Circle, occurring from September to April mainly at coastal locations, especially in the north and east. Snow Buntings feed in tight flocks, creeping along short turf, stubble or shingly seashores, the rear birds periodically fluttering to overtake those at the front and – when they fly – they really do resemble a brief snow flurry. On the ground they can look surprisingly unstriking, as there are usually far more females and juveniles than males. In fact the lovely breeding-plumage male is only likely to be seen on the breeding grounds, or as a very late spring migrant. Nevertheless, no other finch-like bird is so white on the underparts, face and wings. The upperparts have a distinct gingery tinge. The call is an appropriate jingly twittering, and there is also a ringing 'teeu' that is similar to a Lapland Bunting's (see page 235), but a little more drawn out.

Flying flocks really do resemble a flurry of snow. Usually seen in small flocks of fewer than 50 birds. Numbers wintering in Britain vary considerably.

Female (below). Look for Snow Buntings in autumn and winter around the coast, on short-grass fields, rough land and shingly beaches. In winter they feed principally on seeds.

Male (above and left). Long-winged for a bunting, the male becomes progressively whiter as spring approaches. Plumage is most white in late spring. White wing patches and underparts always very distinctive. Variable amount of white on face.

CORN BUNTING *Emberiza calandra*

18CM, 7IN

The largest and – it has to be said – clumsiest looking of the buntings, almost striking in its lack of obvious markings. Both sexes and all ages are dull brown with streaking above and below, but no clear wing bars or face pattern. The bird is often conspicuously perched on a post or wires, where its large, yellowy bill and pink legs are noticeable. Its song is a scratchy jangle, likened to a bunch of keys being shaken. The flight call is a short, liquid 'kwit'. Corn Buntings are well distributed on arable farmland across much of England, but are scarce or absent in the south-west, Wales, Ireland and most of Scotland (except some parts of the east and Outer Hebrides). This patchy distribution is likely to get even patchier, as they seem to be generally declining, probably due to modern farming methods. In winter quite large flocks may be seen and heard flying to their roosts. Corn Buntings are less inclined to join mixed species flocks than other buntings and finches.

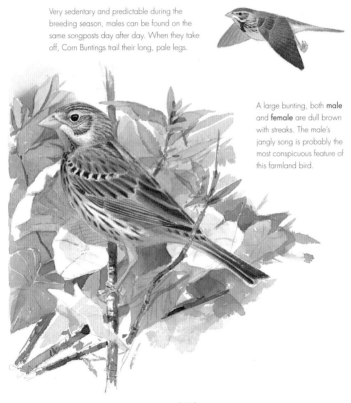

Very sedentary and predictable during the breeding season, males can be found on the same songposts day after day. When they take off, Corn Buntings trail their long, pale legs.

A large bunting, both **male** and **female** are dull brown with streaks. The male's jangly song is probably the most conspicuous feature of this farmland bird.

YELLOWHAMMER *Emberiza citrinella*

16.5CM, 6.5IN

Resident all over Britain, mainly in open country with nearby hedgerows and areas of scrub. The males can be very conspicuous during the early breeding season, when they perch on the tops of bushes and sing their famous 'little bit o' bread and no cheeeese' song. This is, in fact, only the rhythm: the tone is quite thin and metallic, ending with the long drawn-out wheeeze (the 'cheeeese' bit!). Females and juveniles look very similar to female and juvenile Cirl Bunting (see page 235), but Cirl Bunting is a very rare and localized bird. Yellowhammer has a chestnut rump, whereas Cirl Bunting's is brown. Female and juvenile Reed Bunting is also brown and streaky, but has rufous cheeks and a rufous shoulder patch. The flight calls are a metallic 'chip', and a soft 'tillip'.

In flight, the rather long tail and white outer tail feathers are noticeable, as is the bright chestnut rump when the bird takes off in front of you. (Note that several other species also have white outer tails: other buntings, Chaffinches, and larks and pipits.)

Juvenile (above). Out of breeding season, Yellowhammers may well join mixed feeding flocks along with other finches and buntings.

Female (right). Yellowhammers usually nest at the bases of hedges and bushes, often on the ground, the nest partly hidden by grass. They feed on the ground, but often sing from a tree.

Adult male (above). Very yellow indeed, but females and young birds can be rather brown and dull, with the yellow restricted merely to a wash on the face pattern.

REED BUNTING *Emberiza schoeniclus*

15CM, 6IN

Common resident all over Britain. By no means only seen in reeds, although it does often breed near water. In winter it may join other species in mixed flocks of finches and buntings. The male has a black head and bib with a white moustache. Females and juveniles are – inevitably – less boldly marked, being dark brown above with a lot of streaking, as are males in winter. The features that distinguish Reed Bunting from similar streaky buntings are the rufous cheek, outlined in black, and the small rufous patch at the shoulder (compare Yellowhammer, and Cirl and Lapland Buntings). Like several species, Reed Buntings have white outer tail feathers, but these are perhaps even more vivid in this species due to its habit of flicking its tail as it drops into cover. The most common flight calls are a plaintive thin 'tseeee u', and a loud 'tsik'. The song is short and neat, 'chink chink chink chittichink', accelerating into the last phrase. It is usually delivered from a bush or reed-top perch.

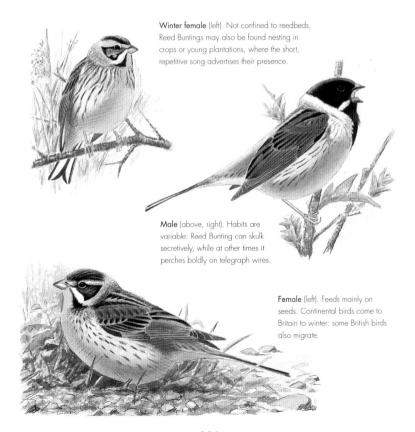

Winter female (left). Not confined to reedbeds, Reed Buntings may also be found nesting in crops or young plantations, where the short, repetitive song advertises their presence.

Male (above, right). Habits are variable: Reed Bunting can skulk secretively, while at other times it perches boldly on telegraph wires.

Female (left). Feeds mainly on seeds. Continental birds come to Britain to winter: some British birds also migrate.

SIMILAR SPECIES: LITTLE BROWN BIRDS

Skulkers and warbler 'impersonators'. Wren, Dunnock and Robin: these three have all been responsible for many a claim of a 'possible' rare warbler. They can all creep and skulk and give only tantalizing glimpses. Robins are particularly versatile, often flicking like chats or fluttering like flycatchers. If you think you are in pursuit of a rarity, ask yourself whether you are sure it isn't just a shy or poorly seen common species.

Wren
A quick flash of its eyestripe can look very warbler-like.

Sedge Warbler
A true eye-striped warbler.

Dunnock
Often shows just a flick of its wings or tail.

Robin
Much less distinctive if seen from behind or in flight, rather than from the front or sides. The red breast isn't always obvious.

Juvenile Stonechat (left). Scaly, with odd patches of orange. Another question worth asking yourself if a bird's plumage doesn't quite seem to fit the book: is it in moult?

Young Robin (above). Red breast only partially developed. Bear in mind that this common species may bear a passing resemblance to rare species.

Male Common Redstart (right). Can look messy like this in both spring and – especially – autumn. In many species both juveniles and adults in 'intermediate' plumages can look scruffy, and therefore confusing.

Lapland Bunting (below). The first step to identification is to make sure what family the bird belongs to, in this case the buntings.

Female Yellowhammer (left). Small birds may shuffle around obscured by stubble or short grass.

Tree Sparrow (left). Some birds show patches of colour or blackish markings.

Skylark (below). If you can see the bill shape, that will be a good start to pinpointing the correct family.

Reed Bunting, non-breeding male (above). In autumn and winter it may be hard to get good views of small birds.

Meadow Pipit (right). Is the bird smooth or streaky?

RARE, ESCAPED & LOCALIZED BIRDS

The following pages show a number of species that are rare, or have most probably escaped from captivity. Some of them are – fortunately – pretty easy to identify, but others can be confused with more common species. Wildfowl collections often include not only 'exotic' ducks and geese, but also species that do occasionally occur in Britain as genuine rarities. A few tell-tale signs may lead you to be suspicious of a bird's credentials. Is it unusually tame? Is it sporting a ring on its leg? Do the tips of its wings look cut short (evidence of wing clipping)? Is it the middle of summer (most genuine rare wildfowl occur in winter)? Even if the bird looks and acts as if it is wild, I'm afraid that's not proof that it really is. Maybe it doesn't matter if it's good to look at. These initial pages include only some of the suspicious wildfowl that you may well come across.

Bar-headed Goose *Anser indicus*
This is always an escape – the species belongs in India. Fortunately, it is not really confusable with any genuine British geese.

Swan Goose *Anser cygnoides*
A farmyard goose that has gone astray. May interbreed with Greylags. The give-away is usually the saggy belly.

Muscovy Duck *Cairina moschata*
Another farmyard wanderer that may join wild ducks, but it is usually tame and dozy, and the weird shape is unmistakable. Also occurs in black and white.

Wood Duck *Aix sponsa*
A native of North America – an escape. Similar looks and habits to Mandarin Duck (see page 15). **Male** (below, left) lacks Mandarin's 'sails', the **female** (below, right) really is very similar.

Chiloe Wigeon *Anas sibilatrix*
A frequent escape. Does not occur wild. Similar shape to Wigeon (see page 16), but male has different head colours. Females are so similar you wouldn't notice them anyway!

RARE, ESCAPED & LOCALIZED BIRDS

Snow Goose *Anser caerulescens*
Wild Snow Geese are found among flocks
of other wild geese (usually Greenland
White-fronted Geese), mainly in Scotland
and Ireland. Snow Geese further south are
probably escapes. Snow Geese seen in
summer certainly are.

Ferruginous Duck *Aythya nyroca*
Very rarely a genuine wild bird. Same kind of inland waters
as Tufted Duck and Common Pochard. Beware female
Tufteds with white undertails, and hybrids between Tufted
and Common Pochard, or even with Ferruginous Duck.

Red-breasted Goose *Branta ruficollis*
A very few genuine wild birds probably occur; those found
with flocks of Brent, Pink-footed or White-fronted Geese
probably have the best credentials. However, the species is
very common in captivity and undoubtedly escapes.

Red-crested Pochard *Netta rufina*
Female (left) and **male** (right). More likely to be
an escape than a genuinely wild bird. Seen
on park lakes, ponds and reservoirs. Beware
confusing female with female Ruddy Duck, Smew
or Common Scoter (see pages 226, 29 and 30).

Ruddy Shelduck *Tadorna ferruginea*
Either an extreme rarity or – far more likely – a
fairly common escape from collections. Largely
apricot coloured, with large white wing patches.
Most confusable with Egyptian Goose.

Egyptian Goose *Alopochen aegyptiaca*
A weird-looking bird that looks more like a large
exotic duck than any of the British geese. Not a wild
species, but a feral population has built up in south-east
England, and it is now accepted on the British list.

RARE, ESCAPED & LOCALIZED BIRDS

King Eider *Somateria spectabilis*
A few individuals occur each year, almost
exclusively off the coast of Scotland or the
Northern Isles, sometimes – though not always
– with Common Eiders. This is a **male**.

Bean Goose *Anser fabalis*
A rare species only found in small
numbers in one or two favoured locations
in Scotland and East Anglia, and it is only
there that you are really likely to see it.

Surf Scoter *Melanitta perspicillata*
Female (left) and **male** (right). Not kept in captivity.
A few occur each winter, mainly off the Scottish
or Irish coasts, usually among flocks of the more
common scoter species (see pages 30–1 for
comparison). Like a Velvet Scoter with all-dark wing.

Spoonbill *Platalea leucorodia*
Most likely at one of the
east-coast bird reserves (e.g.
Minsmere in Suffolk or Cley in
Norfolk) in spring or autumn.
A few also occur in winter,
mainly on southern estuaries.

Ruddy Duck *Oxyura jamaicensis*
Female (top) and **male** (below). Introduced North American
species that some conservationists declared could become
a threat to the highly endangered European White-headed
Duck with which Ruddy Ducks were prone to hybridise.
Whatever the science or morality, a large number of 'British'
Ruddy Ducks were shot and it is now scarce.

Common Crane *Grus grus*
In Britain, migrating cranes are
seen mainly in the south and
east, and the birds have also
now started breeding in eastern
England. Huge and graceful, with
drooping, curved tail feathers and
long legs.

226

RARE, ESCAPED & LOCALIZED BIRDS

White-tailed Eagle *Haliaetus albicilla*
Reintroduction programme in the Western Isles (Hebrides): a few young have been successfully reared. More likely on the ground than Golden Eagle; when it takes off it is like a flying barn door.

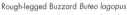

Honey Buzzard *Pernis apivorus*
Much rarer than Common Buzzard. Just a few pairs at well-known but well-protected sites in the southern half of England. Summer visitor. Very variable. Soars on flatter wings than Common Buzzard (see page 67).

Rough-legged Buzzard *Buteo lagopus*
A winter visitor only, almost exclusively to the east coast. Just a few may also pass through the Northern Isles or Scotland in spring on their way to Scandinavian breeding grounds.

Golden Eagle *Aquila chrysaetos*
Biggest native British bird of prey (introduced White-Tailed Sea Eagles, above, are even bigger). Only in Highlands of Scotland and the Western Isles (plus a few individuals in the Lake District). Avoid confusion with much more common Common Buzzard. When you really see an eagle, you'll know it.

RARE, ESCAPED & LOCALIZED BIRDS

Lady Amherst's Pheasant *Chrysolophus amherstiae*
Shown in foreground. Yet another exotic that hardly
qualifies as a wild bird, but there are a few pretending
in southern woodlands. Male dazzlingly obvious.
Female similar to Golden Pheasant but larger.

Golden Pheasant
Chrysolophus pictus
An exotic introduction. Small
numbers almost wild in East
Anglia, Galloway and the
Isles of Scilly, and they might
establish elsewhere. Despite
the **male's** (left) gaudy
plumage, a shy species.

Kentish Plover *Charadrius alexandrinus*
A rare but annual visitor to Britain in small
numbers, most likely in spring and autumn.
Similar coastal habitat to Ringed Plover.
Resembles juvenile Ringed Plover (see
page 81), but note black legs.

Pectoral Sandpiper *Calidris melanotos*
The most frequent American species to
occur this side of the Atlantic. Mainly
recorded in September or October,
especially in Ireland. Usually skulks in
low vegetation in freshwater marshes.

Spotted Crake
Porzana porzana
May not be quite as rare
as we think, but certainly
very hard to see. A few
breed in Britain each year,
deep in marshes. Strange
'whiplash' call. Looks like
a short-billed, spotty Water
Rail (see page 75).

Corncrake *Crex crex*
Scarce summer visitor, breeding only
in the Western Isles of Scotland and in
Ireland. Very occasionally turns up at
coastal sites on migration. Call both
distinctive and relentless, 'crex crex'.

Stone-curlew *Burhinus oedicnemus*
A scarce summer visitor. Small breeding population restricted to
sandy heaths and adjacent farmland in East Anglia and Dorset/
Hampshire. It is shy, secretive and perfectly camouflaged,
especially when it freezes, but once seen it is unmistakable.

RARE, ESCAPED & LOCALIZED BIRDS

Red-necked Phalarope *Phalaropus lobatus*

The characteristic feature of both Red-necked and Grey Phalaropes (see below) is that they habitually feed by swimming on water, spinning round and round picking off flies. Small breeding population is restricted to Shetland, and occasionally seen further south on autumn passage on fresh water (but rarely more than one or two birds).

Breeding plumage (above), non-breeding plumage (above, right), juvenile (right).

Grey Phalarope *Phalaropus fulicarius*

Occurs around Britain's coasts and occasionally inland almost exclusively in autumn, mainly in September and October, but possible any time in winter. It will almost invariably be swimming on the water. The phalarope's dark cap and black eye patch are often surprisingly noticeable. Heavier bill distinguishes a Grey from a Red-necked. Can be very tame.

Juvenile (above, centre) and **non-breeding plumage** (above). Pale grey upperparts variably flecked with darker feathers, and white underparts. These are the only likely plumages to be seen in Britain.

Does not breed in Britain and – as far as I know – **breeding plumage** (top) has never been seen here. A pity, since it is very striking, with totally orange underparts.

RARE, ESCAPED & LOCALIZED BIRDS

Long-tailed Skua *Stercorarius longicaudus*
The rarest of the British skuas. Does not breed here, but in some years quite large numbers are seen on spring migration, mainly off the Hebrides and other northern seawatch points. Alas, not always seen with long tail.

Rock Dove *Columba livia*
Feral pigeons (see page 132) can look exactly like Rock Doves – they descended from them originally. Genuine wild birds probably occur only on the coastal areas of western Scotland and Ireland. Note the pale rump.

Glaucous Gull *Larus hyperboreus*
Non-breeding (left) and **breeding** (right).
A 'white-winged' gull from the Arctic. The larger of the white-winged gulls. Can be as big as a Great Black-backed. Note the heavy beak. Juveniles are biscuit-coloured, second-years almost pure white, adults like large Herring Gull.

Iceland Gull *Larus glaucoides*
Non-breeding (left) and **breeding** (right)
More petite than Glaucous (usually smaller than Herring Gull), with smaller bill and kindlier face. The same range of plumages as Glaucous. Generally the scarcer of the two species.

RARE, ESCAPED & LOCALIZED BIRDS

Snowy Owl *Bubo scandiaca*

An extremely rare Arctic visitor. A pair used to breed on the Shetland Island of Fetlar, but now it is only sporadically recorded. Compare Barn Owl (see page 137). Snowy is much bigger.

Ring-necked Parakeet *Psittacula krameri*

It is a pretty safe assumption that any green parakeet with a long tail making a not entirely pleasant screeching noise is this species. Several colonies of this exotic immigrant from the Himalayas of India are thriving, mainly in the south of England, particularly London. In the mornings and evenings, small squadrons of fast-flying parakeets zoom overhead from or to their roosts.

Hoopoe *Upupa epops*

Hoopoes have very occasionally bred in Britain, but they mainly occur as scarce migrants, usually at coastal sites in spring or autumn, most likely in the south and east. Beware confusion with Jay. Hoopoes fly like huge butterflies.

Bluethroat *Luscinia svecica*

A scarce passage migrant at coastal locations, either in May (especially on the east and north-east coasts) or in September. In autumn birds are likely to be in dull juvenile plumage, without the Union Jack waistcoat.

Wryneck *Jynx torquilla*

Most likely to be seen on migration – especially on the east coast and Northern Isles – in spring, and less commonly in autumn. Technically this is a small woodpecker, but most often seen on the ground or on stone walls.

RARE, ESCAPED & LOCALIZED BIRDS

There are many species of rare warbler that occur very occasionally in Britain as vagrants. Finding and identifying them is a tricky business. On the next two pages are a few that are at least slightly more frequent. Your best chance of seeing any of them is at a coastal migration hot spot in the autumn. With any luck at all, there will be other birders in the area to corroborate – or contradict – your sighting.

Melodious Warbler *Hippolais polygotta* (above)
Icterine Warbler *Hippolais icterina* (left)
These have the jizz of the Reed Warbler types, but plumage is more akin to Willow Warbler's. Rather slow movers. Best distinction is wing length – Icterine has a longer pointed wing.

Pallas's Warbler *Phylloscopus proregulus*
Pallas's in particular may occur quite late in the year. As small as a Goldcrest and a mass of yellowy stripes, most notably on the crown and across the rump.

Yellow-browed Warbler *Phylloscopus inornatus*
Like Pallas's, petite and agile, and most likely at coastal locations in autumn. Yellow-browed has a loud, thin call, 'tsooeeet', like a Coal Tit's, which may draw attention to the bird.

Barred Warbler *Sylvia nisoria*
A clumsy, slow-moving warbler, clearly related to Blackcap and Garden Warbler. Often found in their company. Only breeding birds are barred – we don't see them like this in Britain in autumn. Imagine it without bars.

RARE, ESCAPED & LOCALIZED BIRDS

THREE LOCALIZED BREEDERS

Cetti's Warbler *Cettia cetti*
The original elusive little brown skulking bird.
A small number breed in marshy locations in
southern England. Song: very loud and fruity:
'chip chewicha weecha' (and variants). Once
heard, an easily recognized resident.

Dartford Warbler *Cettia cetti*
This and Cetti's are the only British breeding warblers
that are not summer visitors only. Breeds in heathland
in Hampshire and Dorset, and stays all winter. Best
located by its soft, grating 'chirr' calls or scratchy
song. Generally rather skulky.

Marsh Warbler *Acrocephalus palustris*
Extremely similar to Reed Warbler and difficult to identify
by plumage. Song is very different: a rich jumble of
notes incorporating mimicry of other species. Very scarce
breeder in the south and scarce spring migrant in the
Northern Isles.

RARE, ESCAPED & LOCALIZED BIRDS

Red-breasted Flycatcher *Ficedula parva*
A rare migrant seen very rarely in breeding plumage. Far more likely in autumn. Similar to a female Pied Flycatcher, but note the lack of white wing bar. Imagine this without the red breast. Beware confusion with moulty Stonechats and young Robins.

Crested Tit *Lophophanes cristatus*
Lives only in the mature pine forests of Scotland, and even there it can be hard to find. Outside the breeding season, birds may join other species and rove a little.

Golden Oriole *Oriolus oriolus*
Female (left) and **male** (right). Summer visitors and small numbers breed, mainly in poplar plantations in East Anglia. A few also turn up on migration, most commonly in late spring. Song distinctive – a fluty whistle. May be confused with glimpses of Green Woodpeckers.

Red-backed Shrike *Lanius collurio*
Male (left) and **female** (right). Probably extinct as a breeding bird in Britain, but still occurs in small numbers as a migrant. Your best bet is probably the Northern Isles in May or early June.

RARE, ESCAPED & LOCALIZED BIRDS

Chough *Pyrrhocorax pyrrhocorax*
Resident on rocky coasts in a few places in western
Britain, Ireland and the Isle of Man. Even where
Choughs are present, you are unlikely to see more
than a dozen or so together. Like a Jackdaw with
a curved red bill and 'sneezing' call.

Scottish Crossbill *Loxia scotica*
Defined as a separate species within the last
20 years. Confined to northern Scotland.
Almost impossible to differentiate from Common
Crossbill (see page 215) in the field: Scottish
has a larger beak.

Lapland Bunting *Calcarius lapponicus*
Scarce visitor, mainly to coastal locations, in autumn
and very occasionally spring. Small numbers may
winter in some years on short-cropped terrain. Has
very occasionally bred in Scotland, but usually seen
in winter-type plumage.

Cirl Bunting *Emberiza cirlus*
Male (right) and **female** (left). Very rare in
Britain, breeding only in a few rural areas in
south-west England. Similar to Yellowhammer
(see page 220), but male has a striking
face pattern: black crown, eyeline and chin.
Female has a brown rump.

Ortolan Bunting *Emberiza hortulana*
A few occur in spring (May) and slightly more in
autumn (September). Typical bunting, with white
outer tail feathers, distinctive male, but drab
female and juvenile. All show a white orbital ring.

FURTHER ACTION

Many bird books include a page of 'suggested further reading'. I am a little loath to do this as, frankly, there are an awful lot of excellent books available on all aspects of birds and birdwatching, and – more to the point – new ones are being published all the time. I do, however, suggest that you subscribe to at least two of the various bird magazines on the market. Have a look at them all and decide which ones best suit your taste. In fact, all or any of these magazines can provide the extra information you may need about new books, birdlines, pager services, optical equipment and so on. Above all, I do recommend – nay exhort – you to join a number of conservation organizations. I really believe that anyone who takes pleasure from watching birds is honour bound to help protect them. Please do so.

MAGAZINES

Birdwatch
From newsagents, or from: Birdwatch
(Subscriptions Department),
Fulham House, Goldsworth Road,
Woking, Surrey GU21 lLY.
Tel: 01778 392027
Email: birdwatchsubs@warnersgroup.co.uk

Bird Watching
From newsagents, or from:
Bird Watching (Subscriptions),
Tower House, Sovereign Park, Market
Harborough, Leicestershire LE 16 9EF.
Tel: 0845 601 1356
Email: emap@subscription.co.uk

Birding World
By subscription from:
Stonerunner, Coast Road,
Cley Next the Sea,
Holt, Norfolk NR25 7RZ.
Tel: 01263 741139
Email: sales@birdingworld.co.uk

British Birds
By subscription from:
Production and Circulation,
4 Harlequin Gardens,
St Leonards on Sea, East Sussex TN37 7PF.
Tel: 01424 755155
www.britishbirds.co.uk

BBC Wildlife
From newsagents, or from:
FREEPOST LON 16059,
Sittingbourne, Kent ME9 8DF.
Tel: 0844 844 0251
Email: wildlife@servicehelpline.co.uk

CONSERVATION ORGANIZATIONS

RSPB (The Royal Society
for the Protection of Birds)
The Lodge, Sandy, Bedfordshire SG19 2DI.
Tel: 01767 680551

BTO (British Trust for Ornithology)
The National Centre for Ornithology,
The Nunnery, Thetford, Norfolk IP24 2PU.
Tel: 1842 750050
Email: info@bto.org

The Wildfowl and Wetlands Trust
Slimbridge, Gloucestershire GL2 7BT.
Tel: 1453 891900
Email: enquiries @wwt.org

The Wildlife Trusts
The Kiln, Waterside, Mather Road,
Newark, Nottinghamshire NG24 1WT.
Tel: 01636 677711
Email: enquiry@wildlifetrusts.org

INDEX

Numbers in **bold** refer to
main entries